MASTERING
the Art of
MANAGEMENT

A Step-by-Step Guide to Building Leadership
Skills and Achieving Success as a Manager

SAMUEL VALME, Ph.D.

Mastering The Art of Management

Copyright © 2023 by Samuel Valme

ISBN: 9798378810956

To my dearest wife Jacqueline,

I dedicate this work to you, my love. Throughout my life, you have been my constant source of support, encouragement, and inspiration. Your unwavering love and devotion have been the foundation of our relationship, and I am grateful for every moment we have shared together.

Your kindness, patience, and understanding have always been a guiding light, helping me through difficult times and celebrating with me during the good. I admire your strength, your determination, and your unwavering commitment to our family.

I want to express my deepest gratitude for all that you have done for me, for our children, and for our family. I am honored to be your husband, and I am grateful for the love and joy you bring to my life each day.

Thank you for being my partner, my best friend, and the love of my life. I dedicate this work to you, with all my heart.

CONTENTS

CHAPTER 1: Introduction - Defining the Role And Responsibilities of a Manager...1

    Understanding The Role and Responsibilities of a Manager 3

    Building A Positive and Productive Work Culture 5

    Effective Communication and Relationship Building..............................6

    Navigating The Challenges of Change and Innovation...........................7

    Application 9

    References 10

    Summary 11

CHAPTER 2: Building Self-Awareness and Emotional Intelligence.........12

    Understanding Your Thoughts, Feelings, and Behaviors.......................14

    Figure 1 Three Self-awareness Components 15

    Emotional Intelligence in Action...18

    Figure 2 Emotional Intelligence Components 18

    Enhancing Self-Awareness and Emotional Intelligence........................19

    Application 20

    Summary 21

CHAPTER 3: Communicating Effectively and Developing Strong Relationships..23

    Understanding the Basics of Effective Communication........................24

    Figure 3 Types of Communication..24

    Figure 4 Elements of Effective Communication 25

    Communicating with Your Team...26

    Overcoming Communication Challenges...28

    Application 30

    Summary 32

CHAPTER 4: Motivating and Inspiring Teams to Achieve Goals.............33

    Setting Clear Goals and Expectations 35

    Figure 5 SMART: Specific, Measurable, Achievable, Relevant and Time-Bound.. 36

    Recognition and Rewards 37

Building a Positive and Supportive Work Environment.......................... 38

Application.. 40

Summary.. 41

CHAPTER 5: Setting Objectives and Developing Strategies 42

Identifying and Prioritizing Goals... 44

Developing and Implementing Action Plans............................... 46

Measuring and Evaluating Progress... 47

Strategic Thinking.. 50

Application.. 53

Summary.. 54

CHAPTER 6: Making Decisions and Solving Problems 55

Gather and Analyze Information.. 57

Creativity and Innovation... 60

Managing Uncertainty and Risk.. 63

Application.. 68

Summary.. 69

CHAPTER 7: Managing Time and Prioritizing Tasks............................... 70

Understanding Time Management Techniques and Tools...................... 71

Prioritizing Tasks and Managing Demands................................. 78

Managing Meetings and Communication 81

Maximizing Productivity and Efficiency 83

Overcoming Procrastination and Distractions............................. 85

Application.. 86

Summary.. 88

CHAPTER 8: Building a Positive and Productive Work Culture 90

The Importance of Trust and Respect 91

Effective Communication Strategies.. 96

Strategies for Promoting Work-Life Balance.............................. 98

The Role of Recognition and Rewards 100

Creating a Culture of Learning and Growth 102

Application.. 105

Summary 107

CHAPTER 9: Adapting to Change and Embracing Innovation 108

Cultivating a Growth Mindset 110
The Role of Experimentation in Adapting to Change and Embracing
Innovation 119
Overcoming Resistance to Change 122
Building a Culture of Innovation 124
The Power of Collaboration 126
Application 131
Summary 133

CHAPTER 10: Continuously Improving and Developing as a Manager. 134

Strategies for Personal and Professional Growth as a Manager 136
Maximizing Leadership Potential through Ongoing Development 140
Techniques for Continuous Improvement in Management Skills 144
Staying Ahead of the Curve 146
Cultivating a Growth Mindset 148
Application 154
Summary 155

Figure 1 Three Self-awareness Components 15
Figure 2 Emotional Intelligence Components 18
Figure 3 Types of Communication 24
Figure 4 Elements of Effective Communication 25
Figure 5 SMART: Specfic, Measurable, Achievable, Relevant and Time-
Bound 36

MASTERING
the Art of
MANAGEMENT

A Step-by-Step Guide to Building Leadership
Skills and Achieving Success as a Manager

CHAPTER 1

Introduction - Defining the Role
And Responsibilities of a Manager

In today's fast-paced business environment, managers play a vital role in leading and guiding teams to achieve organizational goals. They are responsible for setting direction, making decisions, and creating a positive work culture that fosters productivity, creativity, and growth.

Being a manager is not an easy task, it requires a unique set of skills and knowledge that can only be acquired through experience and ongoing professional development. This book aims to provide a comprehensive guide to mastering the art of management, covering a wide range of topics that are essential for success in this role.

From building self-awareness and emotional intelligence, to communicating effectively and motivating teams, this book will provide practical strategies and techniques to help managers navigate the challenges of leading and managing others.

In this chapter, we will explore the role and responsibilities of a manager in more detail and discuss the key skills and attributes that are needed to be an effective leader. Whether you are an experienced manager or new to the role, this chapter will provide an overview of what to expect and what is expected of you in this role. We will delve deeper into the specific responsibilities of a manager, including setting direction, creating, and implementing plans and strategies, and making important decisions. We will also discuss the importance of building a positive and productive work culture, and how managers can foster a sense of teamwork and collaboration among their employees.

Another key aspect of being a manager is the ability to effectively communicate and build strong relationships with both internal and external stakeholders. We will explore different communication styles, techniques for giving and receiving feedback, and strategies for building trust and respect with others.

Managers must also be able to motivate and inspire their teams to achieve goals and drive performance. We will discuss different leadership styles and how to adapt them to different situations, as well as ways to create a sense of ownership and accountability among employees.

In addition to these fundamental responsibilities, managers must also be able to navigate the challenges of change and innovation, and continuously improve and develop as leaders. This chapter will provide an overview of these key concepts and how they relate to the role of a manager.

Ultimately, being a manager is a challenging but rewarding role that requires a diverse set of skills and knowledge. By reading this chapter, you will gain a better understanding of the role and responsibilities of a manager, and the key skills and attributes that are needed to be an effective leader.

Understanding The Role and Responsibilities of a Manager

A manager is a person who is responsible for leading and directing a team or organization. The role of a manager can vary depending on the industry and the size of the organization, but some common responsibilities include:

- ◆ Setting direction and goals for the team or organization

- ◆ Developing and implementing plans and strategies

- ◆ Making important decisions

- ◆ Managing and allocating resources

- ◆ Monitoring performance and progress

- ◆ Providing guidance and mentorship to team members

- ◆ Representing the team or organization to external stakeholders

In addition to these specific responsibilities, managers must also be able to lead and inspire their team to achieve goals and drive performance. They must also be able to navigate the challenges of change and innovation, and continuously improve and develop as leaders.

Being a manager requires a unique set of skills and knowledge that can only be acquired through experience and ongoing professional development. Some of the key skills and attributes that are needed to be an effective manager include:

- ◆ Strong leadership and decision-making abilities

- ◆ Excellent communication and interpersonal skills

- ◆ The ability to build and maintain relationships

- ◆ Strong problem-solving and critical thinking skills

- ◆ The ability to adapt to change and think strategically

- ◆ Strong organizational and time management skills

It's important to note that being a manager is not just about being in charge, it's about being a leader who can guide, motivate, and inspire the team to achieve their goals.

As a manager, it is also important to have a clear understanding of the goals of the organization and how the team's work aligns with those goals. By communicating these goals effectively, a manager can ensure that the team is working towards a shared vision and purpose.

Managers also play an important role in the development of their team members, providing guidance, mentorship, and opportunities for professional growth. By fostering a sense of ownership and accountability among employees, managers can create a culture of high-performance and teamwork.

In summary, the role of a manager is multifaceted and complex. It requires a diverse set of skills and knowledge, as well as a strong sense of leadership and the ability to adapt to change. The ability to lead, guide, motivate and inspire the team is what sets a manager apart from a supervisor.

This section has provided an overview of the role and responsibilities of a manager and the key skills and attributes that are needed to be an effective leader. In the next section, we will delve deeper into building a positive and productive work culture.

Building A Positive and Productive Work Culture

A manager's role is not only to lead and direct the team, but also to create a work environment that fosters productivity, creativity, and growth. A positive and productive work culture is essential for the success of any organization, and managers play a critical role in shaping it.

Creating a positive work culture starts with setting clear expectations and goals, and communicating them effectively to the team. Managers should also lead by example, demonstrating the values and behaviors that they want to see in their team members.

One important aspect of building a positive work culture is fostering a sense of teamwork and collaboration among employees. Managers can encourage teamwork by promoting open communication, recognizing, and rewarding team efforts, and providing opportunities for team building activities. Managers should also strive to create an environment that encourages creativity and innovation. This can be achieved by providing resources, tools, and training, as well as giving employees autonomy and freedom to experiment and explore new ideas. Another key aspect of building a positive work culture is recognizing and rewarding employee achievements. Managers should provide regular feedback, both positive and constructive, and recognize and reward employees for their contributions. This can help to build employee engagement, motivation, and commitment to the organization.

A positive work culture also includes providing a safe and healthy working environment. Managers should ensure that the workplace is free of discrimination and harassment, and that employees have access to resources and support to address any concerns.

Creating a positive and productive work culture is not a one-time event, it requires ongoing effort and commitment. Managers should be continuously monitoring the work culture, and making adjustments as needed to maintain a positive and productive environment.

In addition to the benefits for the team and organization, a positive work culture can also have a positive impact on the manager themselves. A positive work culture can help to reduce stress, increase job satisfaction, and improve overall well-being.

In summary, building a positive and productive work culture is a critical part of a manager's role. By creating an environment that fosters teamwork, creativity, and recognition, managers can help to create a culture of high-performance and engagement. In the next section, we will explore the importance of effective communication and relationship building.

Effective Communication and Relationship Building

As a manager, effective communication and relationship building are essential skills for leading and directing a team or organization. These skills are key to building trust and respect with both internal and external stakeholders.

Effective communication is about more than just speaking clearly and concisely, it's about understanding the needs and perspectives of others, and tailoring your message to suit the audience. Managers should be able to communicate effectively in a variety of settings, including one-on-one conversations, team meetings, and presentations to external stakeholders.

One important aspect of effective communication is listening actively. Managers should be able to listen attentively and respond to the concerns and ideas of others. By listening actively, managers can gain a better understanding of the needs and perspectives of their team members and stakeholders, and make more informed decisions.

Managers should also be able to provide regular and constructive feedback. Feedback can be a powerful tool for improving performance and building trust and respect. Managers should be able to give feedback in a way that is clear, specific, and actionable.

Another key aspect of effective communication is building strong relationships. Managers should be able to build and maintain relationships with both internal and external stakeholders. This includes building trust and respect, as well as understanding the needs and perspectives of others. Managers should also be able to build a sense of teamwork and collaboration among employees. This can be achieved by promoting open communication, recognizing, and rewarding team efforts, and providing opportunities for team building activities.

Effective communication and relationship building skills are not only important for the success of the team or organization, but also for the manager's own well-being. Managers who communicate effectively and build strong relationships tend to be more successful and experience less stress.

In summary, effective communication and relationship building are essential skills for managers. By understanding the needs and perspectives of others, and tailoring your message to suit the audience, managers can build trust and respect with both internal and external stakeholders. This can help to create a culture of high-performance and engagement. In the next section, we will explore the importance of adapting to change and embracing innovation.

Navigating The Challenges of Change and Innovation

In today's rapidly changing business environment, managers must be able to adapt to change and embrace innovation in order to stay competitive and achieve organizational goals.

One of the biggest challenges that managers face is the ability to navigate the constant change that is happening in their organizations. This can include changes in technology, market conditions, and organizational structure. Managers must be able to anticipate and respond to change quickly, and lead their teams through the transition process.

Another challenge that managers face is the ability to innovate and think strategically. This means being able to identify new opportunities and create new solutions to problems. Managers must be able to think outside the box and be willing to take risks in order to stay competitive.

To navigate the challenges of change and innovation, managers must be able to develop a strategic mindset. This means being able to think long-term, identify trends and patterns, and make informed decisions. Managers should also be able to create a culture of innovation within their team, by encouraging experimentation and taking calculated risks.

Managers should also be able to build and maintain a strong network of contacts, both within and outside of their organization. This can help to keep managers informed of new trends and developments in their industry, and provide them with new opportunities for growth and innovation.

Another important aspect of adapting to change and innovation is continuous learning and professional development. Managers should be continuously learning new skills and acquiring new knowledge in order to stay current and competitive.

In summary, Navigating the challenges of change and innovation is a critical part of a manager's role. By developing a strategic mindset, creating a culture of innovation, building a strong network, and continuously learning and developing, managers can stay competitive and achieve organizational goals. This chapter has provided an overview of the role and responsibilities of a manager and the key skills and attributes that are needed to be an effective leader.

Application

Assess their current skills and knowledge: Managers should take an honest look at their current skills and knowledge, and identify areas that need improvement. This can help them to create a development plan that focuses on the most critical areas.

Build a positive and productive work culture: Managers can work on building a positive and productive work culture by setting clear expectations and goals, communicating effectively, fostering a sense of teamwork and collaboration, and recognizing and rewarding employee achievements.

Communicate effectively: Managers should work on their communication skills, by actively listening to others, providing regular and constructive feedback, and building strong relationships with both internal and external stakeholders.

Adapt to change and embrace innovation: Managers should continually monitor the changes happening in their organization, think strategically, and be willing to take calculated risks. They can also work on building a culture of innovation within their team.

Continuously learn and develop: Managers should make a commitment to continuous learning and professional development, in order to stay current and competitive. This can include attending workshops, networking with peers, or taking on new roles and responsibilities.

By taking these steps, managers can improve their skills and knowledge, and become more effective leaders. They can also help to create a positive and productive work culture, and lead their team through change and innovation.

References

"The 7 Habits of Highly Effective People" by Stephen Covey - This classic book provides practical and powerful lessons on how to become a more effective leader and manager. It covers topics such as setting priorities, building strong relationships, and leading change.

"Good to Great" by Jim Collins - This bestselling book provides insights into what makes a company truly great, and highlights the importance of having a clear vision, building a strong team, and embracing change.

"Drive: The Surprising Truth About What Motivates Us" by Daniel H. Pink - This book delves into the science of motivation and provides practical insights into how managers can inspire and motivate their team.

"Crucial Conversations: Tools for Talking When Stakes Are High" by Kerry Patterson, Joseph Grenny, Ron McMillan, and Al Switzler - This book provides practical techniques for communicating effectively in high-stakes situations, such as giving and receiving feedback, and resolving conflicts "The Innovator's Dilemma" by Clayton M. Christensen - This book provides insights into how companies can stay competitive and innovative, even in the face of disruptive change.

These books can serve as a great resource for managers who are looking to improve their skills and knowledge, and become more effective leaders. They provide practical strategies, techniques and insights that can be applied to the challenges of management.

Summary

In chapter one, we discussed the various elements that make up the role of a manager and the skills that are essential for success in this role. We highlighted the importance of communication, decision-making, problem-solving, and leadership, as well as the ability to inspire and motivate a team. We also discussed the importance of adaptability and the ability to navigate change and uncertainty. In addition, we provided an overview of the different management styles and the benefits and drawbacks of each. Overall, chapter one provided a comprehensive overview of the key skills and attributes that are necessary for success as a manager, and provided an understanding of the role and its various aspects.

CHAPTER 2

Building Self-Awareness
and Emotional Intelligence

Self-awareness and emotional intelligence are key skills that are essential for success as a manager. Self-awareness is the ability to understand your own thoughts, feelings, and behavior and how they impact others. Emotional intelligence is the ability to recognize and understand emotions in yourself and others, and to use this information to guide your thinking and behavior.

In this chapter, we will explore the importance of self-awareness and emotional intelligence in the role of a manager. We will discuss the different aspects of self-awareness, including self-reflection, self-regulation, and self-motivation, and how they relate to the role of a manager. We will also explore the different aspects of emotional intelligence, including emotional awareness, empathy, and emotional regulation, and how they can be used to build strong relationships, lead teams effectively, and make better decisions.

This chapter will provide practical strategies and techniques for building self-awareness and emotional intelligence, and will explore how these skills can be developed and improved over time. Whether you're an experienced manager or new to the role, this chapter will provide valuable insights and tools for building these essential skills. Self-awareness and emotional intelligence are critical skills for managers because they enable them to understand their own thoughts, feelings, and behavior, and how they impact others. With self-awareness, managers can understand their own strengths and weaknesses, and take steps to improve their performance. Self-awareness also helps managers to be more objective when making decisions and solving problems, and to be more effective in leading and motivating their team.

Emotional intelligence is also essential for managers because it enables them to understand the emotions of others, and to use this information to build strong relationships, lead teams effectively, and make better decisions. For example, by being empathetic, managers can understand the perspectives and needs of their team members, and make decisions that are in the best interest of the team. By being aware of their own emotions, managers can also regulate their own behavior and respond to others in a more effective way.

To build self-awareness and emotional intelligence, managers can use a variety of strategies and techniques. One effective technique is self-reflection, which involves taking time to reflect on your own thoughts, feelings, and behavior and how they impact others. This can help managers to understand their own strengths and weaknesses and to identify areas for improvement.

Another technique for building self-awareness and emotional intelligence is mindfulness, which involves being present in the moment and paying attention to your thoughts, feelings, and sensations.

Mindfulness can help managers to be more self-aware and to be more effective in managing their own emotions and behavior.

Managers can also use emotional intelligence training and coaching, which can provide them with practical tools and techniques for understanding and managing emotions in themselves and others. This can include learning about emotional intelligence theory, practicing emotional intelligence skills, and receiving feedback from a coach.

Self-awareness and emotional intelligence are critical skills for managers. They enable managers to understand their own thoughts, feelings, and behavior, and how they impact others. With self-awareness and emotional intelligence, managers can be more effective in leading and motivating their team, building strong relationships, and making better decisions. Developing Self-Awareness

Understanding Your Thoughts, Feelings, and Behaviors

Self-awareness is the ability to understand one's own thoughts, feelings, and behaviors and how they impact others. It is a critical skill for managers as it enables them to understand their own strengths and weaknesses, and to make more informed decisions.

Self-awareness can be broken down into three main components: self-reflection, self-regulation, and self-motivation.

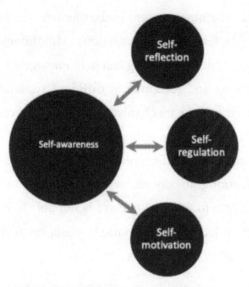

Figure 1 Three Self-awareness Components

Self-reflection is the process of taking time to reflect on one's own thoughts, feelings, and behaviors. It involves looking at oneself objectively and identifying areas for improvement. This can include analyzing past decisions and actions, and considering how they may have impacted others. By engaging in self-reflection, managers can gain a better understanding of their own strengths and weaknesses, and take steps to improve their performance. This can include setting goals and working towards achieving them, seeking feedback from others, and learning from past experiences. Self-reflection can be done through journaling, meditating, or talking with a mentor or coach. It's important to make regular self-reflection a part of the routine, it could be weekly or monthly, to ensure that it becomes a habit and it will be more effective in improving one's self-awareness. Self-regulation is the ability to control one's own thoughts, feelings, and behaviors in response to different situations. It involves being aware of one's own emotions and being able to manage them effectively. This can include techniques such as mindfulness, which can help managers to be more present in the moment and to be more aware of their own thoughts, feelings, and sensations. Mindfulness practices such as meditation, yoga, or deep breathing can help managers to be more aware of their own emotions and reactions to different situations. In addition, developing effective coping mechanisms such as exercise, talking to a friend, or writing down one's thoughts can help managers to regulate their emotions and reactions. Self-regulation also involves setting clear boundaries and learning to say no when necessary to avoid burnout. Managers who are able to self-regulate are better able to handle stress and pressure, make better decisions, and build stronger relationships with their team members and other stakeholders.

Self-motivation is the ability to set and achieve personal goals. It involves having a clear understanding of one's own values, interests, and passions and using that knowledge to set goals and work towards achieving them. Self-motivated managers are driven by their own values and interests, and are less likely to be swayed by external pressures or influences. They are more likely to be persistent in the face of challenges and setbacks and to take initiative when opportunities arise.

To develop self-motivation, managers should start by identifying their own values, interests, and passions. Once they have a clear understanding of what is important to them, they can set specific, measurable, and achievable goals that align with these values and interests. They can also use visualization and positive affirmations to keep themselves motivated and focused on achieving their goals.

Managers can also increase their self-motivation by setting realistic deadlines, breaking down larger goals into smaller, more manageable steps, and celebrating small wins along the way. They can also find accountability partners or join a support group to stay motivated and on track.

Self-motivation is the ability to set and achieve personal goals by using one's own values, interests, and passions as a guide. It's a key aspect of self-awareness and can help managers to be more persistent, take initiative, and achieve their goals. By developing self-motivation, managers can be more effective in achieving their goals, leading, and motivating their team, and building strong relationships with stakeholders.

Managers who have a high level of self-awareness are better equipped to make decisions that are in the best interest of the team, and are better able to lead and motivate others. They are also better able to build strong relationships with their team members and other stakeholders.

Developing self-awareness is a continuous process that requires ongoing effort and commitment. Managers can work on building self-awareness by practicing self-reflection, self-regulation, and self-motivation. This can include setting aside time each day for self-reflection, practicing mindfulness and other emotional regulation techniques, and setting and working towards personal goals.

In addition, managers can also seek feedback from others, such as team members, colleagues, or a coach, to gain a better understanding of how they are perceived by others. This can provide valuable insights into one's own strengths and weaknesses, and help to identify areas for improvement. Self-awareness is a critical skill for managers. It enables managers to understand their own thoughts, feelings, and behaviors and how they impact others. By developing self-awareness through self-reflection, self-regulation, and self-motivation, managers can improve their ability to make decisions, lead and motivate their team, and build strong relationships with stakeholders. In the next section, we will explore the importance of emotional intelligence in the role of a manager.

Emotional Intelligence in Action

Building Strong Relationships and Leading Teams Effectively

Emotional intelligence is the ability to recognize and understand emotions in yourself and others, and to use this information to guide your thinking and behavior. It is a critical skill for managers as it enables them to build strong relationships with their team members and other stakeholders, lead teams effectively, and make better decisions.

Emotional intelligence can be broken down into four main components: emotional awareness, empathy, emotional regulation, and social skills.

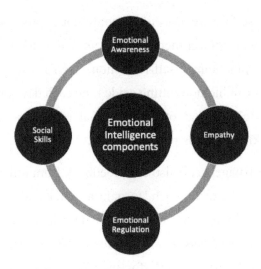

Figure 1 Emotional Intelligence Components

Emotional awareness is the ability to recognize and understand one's own emotions, as well as the emotions of others. It involves being able to identify emotions, understand their causes, and respond to them in an appropriate way. By being emotionally aware, managers can better understand the perspectives and needs of their team members, and make decisions that are in the best interest of the team.

Empathy is the ability to understand and share the feelings of others. It involves being able to put oneself in the shoes of others, and to understand their perspectives and feelings. By being empathetic, managers can build stronger relationships with their team members, and create a more positive and productive work culture. Emotional regulation is the ability to control and manage one's own emotions, as well as the emotions of others. It involves being able to manage stress and pressure, and to respond to difficult situations in a calm and composed manner. By being able to regulate their own emotions, managers can be more effective in leading and motivating their team, and in making important decisions.

Social skills are the ability to effectively communicate and interact with others. It involves being able to build strong relationships, communicate effectively, and resolve conflicts.

Enhancing Self-Awareness and Emotional Intelligence
Techniques and Strategies for Growth and Development

Self-awareness and emotional intelligence are essential skills for managers, and they can be developed and enhanced over time. Managers can use a variety of techniques and strategies to improve their self-awareness and emotional intelligence and become more effective leaders.

One effective technique for building self-awareness and emotional intelligence is mindfulness. Mindfulness is the practice of being present in the moment and paying attention to your thoughts, feelings, and sensations. Mindfulness practices such as meditation, yoga, or deep breathing can help managers to be more aware of their own thoughts, feelings, and sensations, and to be more self-aware. Mindfulness can also help managers to regulate their emotions, and to manage stress and pressure more effectively.

Another technique for building self-awareness and emotional intelligence is emotional intelligence training and coaching. Emotional intelligence training and coaching can provide managers with practical tools and techniques for understanding and managing emotions in themselves and others. This can include learning about emotional intelligence theory, practicing emotional intelligence skills, and receiving feedback from a coach.

Managers can also seek feedback from others, such as team members, colleagues, or a coach, to gain a better understanding of how they are perceived by others. This can provide valuable insights into one's own strengths and weaknesses, and help to identify areas for improvement.

Managers can also develop self-awareness and emotional intelligence by setting aside time for self-reflection, reading books and articles on the topic, and by participating in workshops or classes.

In addition, managers can improve their emotional intelligence by practicing empathy, by actively listening to others, and by seeking to understand their perspectives. They can also work on building their social skills by communicating effectively, building strong relationships, and resolving conflicts.

Application

In order to apply the knowledge and insights gained from chapter two, managers can take the following steps:

Develop a regular self-reflection practice: Managers should take time to reflect on their own thoughts, feelings, and behaviors, and how they impact others. This can include setting aside time each day for self-reflection, analyzing past decisions and actions, and seeking feedback from others.

Practice mindfulness: Managers can practice mindfulness techniques such as meditation, yoga, or deep breathing to be more present in the moment, and to be more aware of their own thoughts, feelings, and sensations. This can help managers to be more self-aware and to regulate their emotions more effectively. Seek emotional intelligence training and coaching: Managers can seek out emotional intelligence training and coaching to gain practical tools and techniques for understanding and managing emotions in themselves and others. This can include learning about emotional intelligence theory, practicing emotional intelligence skills, and receiving feedback from a coach.

Seek feedback from others: Managers can seek feedback from team members, colleagues, or a coach to gain a better understanding of how they are perceived by others. This can provide valuable insights into one's own strengths and weaknesses, and help to identify areas for improvement.

Practice empathy: Managers can practice empathy by actively listening to others, seeking to understand their perspectives, and by building strong relationships with their team members and other stakeholders.

By taking these steps, managers can improve their self-awareness and emotional intelligence and become more effective leaders.

Summary

In chapter two, we explored the importance of self-awareness and emotional intelligence in the role of a manager. We discussed the different aspects of self-awareness, including self-reflection, self-regulation, and self-motivation, and how they relate to the role of a manager. We also explored the different aspects of emotional intelligence, including emotional awareness, empathy, emotional regulation, and social skills, and how they can be used to build strong relationships, lead teams effectively, and make better decisions.

We also provided practical strategies and techniques for building self-awareness and emotional intelligence, and discussed how these skills can be developed and improved over time. In summary, chapter two emphasizes the significance of self-awareness and emotional intelligence in the management field and how they can be developed and enhanced to become an effective leader.

CHAPTER 3

Communicating Effectively and Developing Strong Relationships

C hapter three will delve into the topic of communication, one of the most essential skills for managers. Effective communication is a key element of successful leadership and is essential for building strong relationships, leading teams effectively, and achieving organizational goals. In this chapter, we will explore the different types of communication, the importance of effective communication in the workplace, and strategies for improving communication skills. We will also discuss the challenges that managers may face when communicating with team members, colleagues, and other stakeholders, and provide strategies for overcoming these challenges. By the end of this chapter, readers will have a better understanding of the importance of communication in the role of a manager and will be equipped with the tools and strategies needed to improve their own communication skills.

Understanding the Basics of Effective Communication

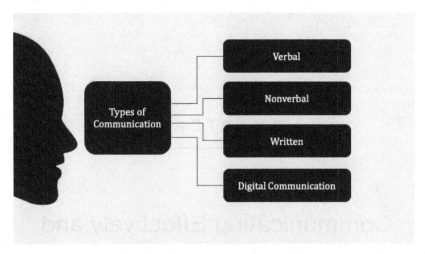

Figure 2 Types of Communication

Effective communication is one of the most essential skills for managers, as it is key to building strong relationships, leading teams effectively, and achieving organizational goals. In order to be an effective communicator, managers must understand the basics of communication, including the different types of communication, the elements of effective communication, and the importance of active listening.

There are several different types of communication, including verbal, nonverbal, written, and digital communication. Verbal communication is the use of spoken words to convey information, while nonverbal communication is the use of body language, facial expressions, and tone of voice to convey meaning. Written communication includes emails, letters, and other written documents, while digital communication includes communication through social media, instant messaging, and other online platforms.

The elements of effective communication include a clear message, appropriate language, and effective delivery. A clear message is one that is easy to understand and is relevant to the audience. Appropriate language is language that is appropriate for the audience and the situation. Effective delivery is the ability to deliver the message in a way that is engaging and effective.

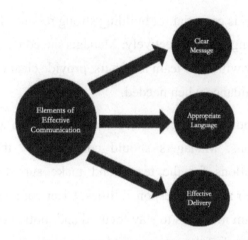

Figure 3 Elements of Effective Communication

Active listening is an important aspect of effective communication. It involves paying attention to what the other person is saying, acknowledging the message, and providing feedback. Active listening can help managers to better understand the perspectives of others and to build stronger relationships with their team members and other stakeholders.

Effective communication is a key element of successful leadership and is essential for building strong relationships, leading teams effectively, and achieving organizational goals. Understanding the basics of communication, including the different types of communication, the elements of effective communication, and the importance of active listening, is essential for managers who want to improve their communication skills. In the next section, we will explore the importance of effective communication in the workplace and the strategies for improving communication skills.

Communicating with Your Team

Building Strong Relationships and Leading Effectively

Effective communication is essential for building strong relationships with team members and leading teams effectively. Managers need to be able to communicate effectively with their team members, provide clear direction, and offer support and guidance when needed.

One of the most important aspects of communicating with a team is setting clear expectations. Managers should communicate the goals, objectives, and expectations for the team, and make sure that team members understand their roles and responsibilities. Clear communication of expectations helps team members to stay focused and motivated, and to understand what is expected of them.

Managers also need to be able to provide clear direction and guidance to their team members. This includes communicating the steps that need to be taken to achieve goals, providing feedback on performance, and offering support and resources when needed. Clear direction and guidance can help team members to stay on track, and to feel supported and motivated.

Managers also need to be able to provide feedback, both positive and negative, in a constructive and supportive manner. Feedback should be given in a timely manner, and should be specific, actionable, and focused on the behavior or task, rather than the person.

Managers should also make an effort to build strong relationships with their team members. This includes creating a positive and supportive work environment, encouraging team members to share their thoughts and ideas, and taking the time to get to know team members on a personal level. Strong relationships with team members can help to build trust, increase motivation, and improve team performance.

Effective team building activities can help to improve communication, build trust and relationships, and increase motivation and productivity within a team. Some examples of effective team building activities include:

Team building retreats: Organizing a team building retreat can provide an opportunity for team members to bond, build relationships, and learn more about each other outside of the workplace. This can include activities such as team-building exercises, problem-solving activities, and outdoor activities.

Virtual team-building activities: With remote working becoming more common, virtual team-building activities can be a great way to connect team members and build relationships. This can include virtual coffee breaks, virtual happy hours, or even virtual escape rooms.

Volunteer work: Participating in volunteer work as a team can help to build a sense of camaraderie and teamwork while also giving back to the community.

Cross-functional team building: Bringing team members from different departments or functions together for a project or task can help to break down silos and build relationships across the organization.

Outdoor activities: Outdoor activities such as hiking, rock climbing, or team sports can help team members to bond and build relationships in a fun and relaxed environment.

Professional development opportunities: Offering professional development opportunities such as workshops, training, or mentoring programs can help team members to build new skills and improve communication within the team.

These are just a few examples of effective team-building activities that can help to improve communication, build trust and relationships, and increase motivation and productivity within a team. It's important for managers to find the right balance of activities that will work for their team.

Finally, in order to lead effectively, managers must be able to communicate well with other stakeholders, including colleagues, customers, and management. This includes being able to clearly articulate the team's objectives and progress, as well as being able to negotiate and resolve conflicts.

In summary, communicating effectively with a team is essential for building strong relationships and leading effectively. Managers should set clear expectations, provide clear direction and guidance, give constructive feedback, build strong relationships with team members, and communicate effectively with other stakeholders to achieve goals and build a successful team.

Overcoming Communication Challenges

Strategies for Success

As a manager, you will inevitably face communication challenges in the workplace. Whether it's communicating with a remote team, dealing with difficult team members, or navigating cultural differences, effective communication is essential for overcoming these challenges and achieving success.

One common challenge that managers face is communicating with a remote team. Remote teams can often rely heavily on digital communication tools such as email, instant messaging, and video conferencing, which can make it difficult to convey tone, intent, and emotions. Without the ability to see facial expressions or body language, it can be harder to gauge the emotional state of team members and to understand their perspectives.

Furthermore, the lack of face-to-face interaction and the inability to read body language can make it harder to build trust and strong relationships with team members. To overcome this challenge, managers should make use of video conferencing to facilitate face-to-face interactions, schedule regular check-ins, and set clear communication protocols. They should also be mindful of the tone and language they use when communicating digitally, and be aware of the potential for miscommunication.

Additionally, remote working also means that team members may be working in different time zones, which can make scheduling meetings and communicating in real-time more difficult.

Managers need to be aware of the potential challenges and take steps to mitigate them, such as using video conferencing to facilitate face-to-face interactions, encouraging regular check-ins, and setting clear communication protocols. They also need to be more mindful of the tone and language they use when communicating digitally, and to be more aware of the potential for miscommunication. They can also use additional means of communication like regular team building activities, or virtual coffee breaks to help build connections.

Another challenge that managers may face is dealing with difficult team members. Difficult team members can be those who are resistant to change, have negative attitudes, or struggle with communication. To overcome this challenge, managers should address the issue directly, provide clear feedback, and set clear expectations. They should also be patient, understanding, and empathetic, and seek to understand the underlying reasons for the difficult behavior.

Managers may also face communication challenges when working with team members from different cultures. Different cultures can have different communication styles and ways of expressing themselves. To overcome this challenge, managers should be aware of cultural differences, and make an effort to understand and respect these differences. They should also encourage team members to share their perspectives and ideas, and provide training on cross-cultural communication. Finally, managers may face communication challenges when dealing with conflicts and disagreements. Conflicts can arise between team members, or between different departments or stakeholders. To overcome this challenge, managers should encourage open communication, provide opportunities for team members to share their perspectives, and seek to understand the underlying reasons for the conflict. They should also be prepared to act as a mediator, and be able to come up with effective solutions to resolve the conflict.

Effective communication is essential for overcoming communication challenges and achieving success as a manager. Managers can use a variety of strategies to overcome communication challenges, including being mindful of the tone and language they use when communicating digitally, addressing issues directly, being patient and empathetic, understanding cultural differences and being prepared to act as a mediator.

Application

In order to apply the knowledge and insights gained from chapter three, managers can take the following steps:

Practice active listening: Managers should practice active listening by paying attention to what others are saying, acknowledging their message, and providing feedback. This will help them to build stronger relationships with their team members and other stakeholders.

Communicate clearly and consistently: Managers should communicate their goals, objectives, and expectations for the team clearly and consistently. This will help team members to understand their roles and responsibilities and to stay focused and motivated.

Provide feedback: Managers should provide feedback, both positive and negative, in a constructive and supportive manner. Feedback should be given in a timely manner, and should be specific, actionable, and focused on the behavior or task, rather than the person.

Build strong relationships: Managers should make an effort to build strong relationships with their team members. This includes creating a positive and supportive work environment, encouraging team members to share their thoughts and ideas, and taking the time to get to know team members on a personal level.

Communicate effectively with remote teams: Managers should make use of video conferencing to facilitate face-to-face interactions, schedule regular check-ins, and set clear communication protocols. They should also be mindful of the tone and language they use when communicating digitally, and be aware of the potential for miscommunication.

Be aware of cultural differences: Managers should be aware of cultural differences and make an effort to understand and respect these differences. They should also encourage team members to share their perspectives and ideas, and provide training on cross-cultural communication.

By taking these steps, managers can improve their communication skills, build stronger relationships with their team members and other stakeholders, and effectively lead their teams.

Summary

In chapter three, we explored the topic of communication, one of the most essential skills for managers. We explored the different types of communication, the importance of effective communication in the workplace, and strategies for improving communication skills. We also discussed the challenges that managers may face when communicating with team members, colleagues, and other stakeholders, and provided strategies for overcoming these challenges. We highlighted the importance of active listening, setting clear expectations, providing clear direction and guidance, giving constructive feedback, building strong relationships with team members, and communicating effectively with other stakeholders. In summary, chapter three provided an in-depth understanding of the importance of communication in the role of a manager, and provided practical strategies and techniques for improving communication skills.

CHAPTER 4

Motivating and
Inspiring Teams to Achieve Goals

M otivating and inspiring teams to achieve goals is a crucial aspect of a manager's role. A motivated and inspired team is more productive, more engaged, and more likely to achieve their goals. In this chapter, we will explore the different strategies and techniques that managers can use to motivate and inspire their teams. We will discuss the importance of setting clear goals, providing recognition and rewards, creating a positive and supportive work environment, and fostering a culture of collaboration and innovation. We will also delve into the concept of emotional intelligence and how it can be used to connect with team members and understand their needs. We will explore various motivational theories and how they can be applied in the workplace. By the end of this chapter, readers will have a better understanding of the importance of motivation and inspiration in the workplace, and will be equipped with the tools and strategies they need to motivate and inspire their teams to achieve their goals.

Motivating and inspiring teams to achieve goals is essential for a manager's success. A motivated and inspired team is more productive, more engaged, and more likely to achieve their goals. In order to motivate and inspire a team, managers must first set clear goals that align with the organization's overall mission and vision. Setting clear goals helps team members to understand what is expected of them and to stay focused on achieving success. Another important aspect of motivating and inspiring teams is providing recognition and rewards. Managers should recognize the hard work and achievements of their team members, and provide rewards that are meaningful and motivating. This can include bonuses, promotions, or other incentives.

Creating a positive and supportive work environment is also crucial for motivating and inspiring teams. Managers should foster a culture of collaboration, where team members feel supported and encouraged to share their ideas and perspectives. They should also create an environment where team members feel valued and respected.

Fostering a culture of innovation is another key aspect of motivating and inspiring teams. Managers should encourage their team members to think creatively and to come up with new ideas that can help the organization to achieve its goals.

Emotional intelligence is also key when it comes to motivating and inspiring teams. Managers with high emotional intelligence are able to connect with their team members and understand their needs. They are able to communicate effectively and to build strong relationships with their team members.

Finally, managers should also be aware of various motivational theories and how they can be applied in the workplace. For example, Maslow's Hierarchy of Needs can help managers to understand the different needs of their team members and to create a work environment that meets those needs.

Motivating and inspiring teams to achieve goals is a crucial aspect of a manager's role. Managers must set clear goals, provide recognition and rewards, create a positive and supportive work environment, foster a culture of innovation and emotional intelligence, and be aware of motivational theories.

Setting Clear Goals and Expectations

The foundation of motivation

The first step in motivating and inspiring teams to achieve goals is setting clear and specific goals. Managers should ensure that the goals they set align with the organization's overall mission and vision. Clear goals help team members to understand what is expected of them, and to stay focused on achieving success.

When setting goals, managers should also ensure that they are SMART: Specific, Measurable, Achievable, Relevant, and Time-bound. This will help to ensure that the goals are clear and achievable, and that progress can be tracked and measured. Managers should also set realistic and challenging goals, as this can help to increase motivation and engagement.

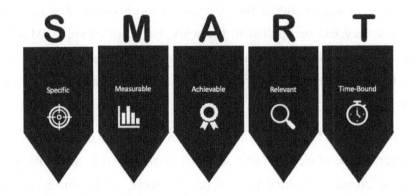

Figure 4 SMART: Specific, Measurable, Achievable, Relevant and Time-Bound

Managers should also provide clear expectations for team members, including what is expected of them, their roles, and responsibilities, and how their performance will be evaluated. This will help to ensure that team members understand their roles and are able to work effectively towards achieving the goals.

Managers should also communicate the goals clearly and consistently to all team members, and encourage them to share their thoughts and ideas. This will help to ensure that all team members are on the same page and are working towards the same goals.

Managers should also provide regular updates on progress and performance, and make adjustments as needed. This will help to ensure that goals are being met and that the team is on track to achieve success.

Setting clear goals and expectations is the foundation of motivation. Managers should set SMART goals that align with the organization's overall mission and vision, provide clear expectations for team members, communicate goals clearly and consistently, encourage team members to share their thoughts and ideas, and provide regular updates on progress and performance. By doing so, they will help to ensure that their teams stay motivated and focused on achieving success.

Recognition and Rewards

Achieving success through appreciation

Recognition and rewards are an important aspect of motivating and inspiring teams to achieve goals. Managers should recognize the hard work and achievements of their team members, and provide rewards that are meaningful and motivating. This can include bonuses, promotions, or other incentives.

Managers should also recognize the contributions of all team members, not just the top performers. This will help to create a sense of fairness and equity, and will ensure that all team members feel valued and appreciated.

Managers should also be aware of different types of recognition and rewards, and how they can be used effectively. For example, public recognition can be a powerful motivator, while more personal forms of recognition such as a handwritten note or a one-on-one conversation can be more meaningful and effective.

Managers should also recognize the importance of non-monetary rewards such as flexible working hours, training and development opportunities, and other forms of recognition, such as employee of the month. These types of rewards can be just as effective in motivating and inspiring teams. Managers should also be mindful of the timing of recognition and rewards, and that they should be given in a timely manner. Waiting too long to recognize or reward an employee can diminish the impact and significance of the recognition.

Recognition and rewards are an important aspect of motivating and inspiring teams to achieve goals. Managers should recognize the hard work and achievements of their team members, and provide rewards that are meaningful and motivating. They should also recognize the contributions of all team members, be aware of different types of recognition and rewards, and be mindful of the timing of recognition and rewards. By doing so, they can help to create a culture of appreciation and help their teams to achieve success.

Building a Positive and Supportive Work Environment

Fostering collaboration and innovation

Creating a positive and supportive work environment is crucial for motivating and inspiring teams. Managers should foster a culture of collaboration, where team members feel supported and encouraged to share their ideas and perspectives. They should also create an environment where team members feel valued and respected.

One way to foster collaboration and a positive work environment is to encourage open communication. Managers should create opportunities for team members to share their thoughts and ideas, and should actively listen to and consider their input. This will help to ensure that all team members feel heard and valued.

Managers should also provide regular training and development opportunities for team members. This will help to ensure that they have the skills and knowledge they need to be successful, and will also help to keep them motivated and engaged.

Managers should also create a culture of innovation by encouraging team members to think creatively and to come up with new ideas that can help the organization to achieve its goals. This can be done by creating opportunities for brainstorming and idea generation, and by providing resources and support for experimentation and experimentation.

Managers should also lead by example, by being positive, supportive, and collaborative themselves. This will help to create a culture of positivity and support, and will inspire team members to do the same.

Building a positive and supportive work environment is crucial for motivating and inspiring teams. Managers should foster a culture of collaboration, where team members feel supported and encouraged to share their ideas and perspectives. They should also create an environment where team members feel valued and respected, encourage open communication, provide regular training and development opportunities, foster a culture of innovation, and lead by example. By doing so, they can help to create a positive and supportive work environment that will foster collaboration and innovation and help their teams to achieve success.

Application

In order to apply the knowledge and insights gained from the chapter on motivating and inspiring teams to achieve goals, managers can take the following steps:

1. Set clear and specific goals that align with the organization's overall mission and vision, and make sure they are SMART (Specific, Measurable, Achievable, Relevant, and Time-bound). Provide clear expectations for team members, including what is expected of them, their roles, and responsibilities, and how their performance will be evaluated.

2. Communicate goals clearly and consistently to all team members, and encourage them to share their thoughts and ideas.

3. Provide regular updates on progress and performance, and make adjustments as needed.

4. Recognize the hard work and achievements of team members, and provide rewards that are meaningful and motivating.

5. Recognize the contributions of all team members, not just the top performers.

6. Be aware of different types of recognition and rewards, and how they can be used effectively.

7. Foster a culture of collaboration and innovation by encouraging team members to think creatively and to share their ideas.

8. Provide regular training and development opportunities for team members.

9. Lead by example, by being positive, supportive, and collaborative yourself.

By taking these steps, managers can create a positive and supportive work environment that will foster collaboration and innovation and help their teams to achieve success. They will be able to set clear goals, provide clear expectations, communicate effectively, and recognize and reward the efforts of their team members, which will ultimately lead to a motivated and inspired team that is more productive, more engaged, and more likely to achieve their goals.

Summary

The chapter on motivating and inspiring teams to achieve goals discussed the importance of motivation and inspiration in the workplace, and provided practical strategies and techniques for motivating and inspiring teams. The chapter began by highlighting the importance of setting clear goals and expectations, which serve as the foundation of motivation. It also discussed the importance of recognition and rewards, highlighting that they are a crucial aspect of motivating and inspiring teams to achieve goals. Managers should recognize the hard work and achievements of their team members and provide rewards that are meaningful and motivating. The chapter also discussed the importance of building a positive and supportive work environment, fostering collaboration and innovation, and the importance of emotional intelligence and how it can be used to connect with team members and understand their needs. The chapter also provided practical tips for applying the knowledge and insights gained, such as setting clear goals, providing clear expectations, recognizing, and rewarding team members efforts, fostering collaboration and innovation, and leading by example. Overall, the chapter emphasized the importance of motivation and inspiration in the workplace, and provided practical strategies and techniques for motivating and inspiring teams to achieve goals.

CHAPTER 5

Setting Objectives and Developing Strategies

In this chapter, we will focus on the importance of setting objectives and developing strategies for achieving success in the role of a manager. Setting objectives and developing strategies is essential for managers, as it allows them to align their efforts with the overall goals and mission of the organization, and to make informed decisions that will help to achieve success. We will explore the process of setting objectives and developing strategies, including how to identify and prioritize goals, how to develop and implement effective action plans, and how to measure and evaluate progress. We will also discuss the importance of strategic thinking and the role it plays in the decision-making process. By the end of this chapter, readers will have a better understanding of the significance of setting objectives and developing strategies, and will be equipped with the tools and strategies needed to set objectives and develop strategies that will help to achieve success in the role of a manager.

Setting objectives and developing strategies is a critical aspect of a manager's role. It allows managers to align their efforts with the overall goals and mission of the organization and make informed decisions that will help to achieve success. When setting objectives and developing strategies, it is important to identify and prioritize goals that are important to the organization This can be done by conducting a SWOT analysis, which helps to identify the organization's strengths, weaknesses, opportunities, and threats. Once the goals have been identified, managers can develop and implement effective action plans that will help to achieve the goals.

An effective action plan should include specific, measurable, and achievable steps that will help to achieve the goals. It should also include a timeline for completion and a plan for monitoring and evaluating progress. To measure and evaluate progress, managers can use a variety of tools such as performance metrics, key performance indicators and progress reports.

Strategic thinking is also an important aspect of setting objectives and developing strategies. It involves thinking about the long-term direction of the organization and considering how to adapt to changing circumstances. This can help managers to anticipate and respond to changes in the business environment and make decisions that will help to achieve success.

Setting objectives and developing strategies is a critical aspect of a manager's role. It allows managers to align their efforts with the overall goals and mission of the organization and make informed decisions that will help to achieve success. By identifying and prioritizing goals, developing, and implementing effective action plans, measuring, and evaluating progress, and using strategic thinking, managers can set objectives and develop strategies that will help to achieve success.

Identifying and Prioritizing Goals

The foundation of success

The first step in setting objectives and developing strategies is to identify and prioritize goals. Managers should ensure that the goals they set align with the overall mission and vision of the organization. This will help to ensure that the goals are in line with the organization's overall direction and will contribute to achieving success.

One effective way to identify and prioritize goals is to conduct a SWOT analysis. SWOT analysis is a tool that helps to identify the organization's strengths, weaknesses, opportunities, and threats. This can help managers to identify areas where the organization can improve and opportunities for growth.

Conducting a SWOT analysis is a useful tool for managers to identify and prioritize goals. SWOT analysis helps to identify the organization's strengths, weaknesses, opportunities, and threats. This can help managers to identify areas where the organization can improve and opportunities for growth.

To conduct a SWOT analysis, managers should first identify the organization's strengths, which are the positive attributes that give the organization an advantage over its competitors. Examples of strengths could be a strong brand reputation, a skilled workforce, or a proprietary technology.

Next, managers should identify the organization's weaknesses, which are the negative attributes that place the organization at a disadvantage. Examples of weaknesses could be a lack of diversification, outdated technology, or a lack of skilled workforce.

Then, managers should identify opportunities, which are external factors that the organization can capitalize on to achieve its goals. Examples of opportunities could be a growing market, new technologies or a change in government regulations.

Finally, managers should identify threats, which are external factors that could negatively impact the organization's performance. Examples of threats could be new competitors entering the market, changes in consumer preferences or economic downturns.

Once the SWOT analysis is complete, managers should prioritize the goals based on the information gathered. For example, if the organization has a weakness in a certain area, such as a lack of diversification, the manager may prioritize goals to address that weakness.

It is important to note that SWOT analysis should be conducted regularly as the organization's strengths, weaknesses, opportunities, and threats can change over time.

A SWOT analysis is a useful tool for managers to identify and prioritize goals by identifying the organization's strengths, weaknesses, opportunities, and threats. By conducting a SWOT analysis, managers can prioritize goals based on the information gathered, and make informed decisions that will help to achieve success. It's important to note that SWOT analysis should be conducted regularly as the organization's strengths, weaknesses, opportunities, and threats can change over time.

When identifying and prioritizing goals, managers should also consider the resources available to them, such as time, budget, and personnel. This will help to ensure that the goals are realistic and achievable within the given constraints.

Managers should also consider the impact of the goals on different stakeholders, such as employees, customers, shareholders, and the community. This will help to ensure that the goals are in line with the organization's values and will contribute to the well-being of all stakeholders.

Once the goals have been identified and prioritized, managers should communicate them clearly and consistently to all team members. This will help to ensure that all team members understand the goals and are working towards the same objectives.

Identifying and prioritizing goals is the foundation of success. Managers should align the goals with the overall mission and vision of the organization, conduct a SWOT analysis to identify areas for improvement and opportunities for growth, consider the resources available to them, consider the impact of the goals on different stakeholders and communicate the goals clearly and consistently to all team members. By doing so, they can help to ensure that their teams are working towards the same objectives and that they are in line with the overall direction of the organization, which will ultimately lead to success.

Developing and Implementing Action Plans

Putting goals into action

Once goals have been identified and prioritized, the next step for managers is to develop and implement action plans. Action plans are specific, measurable, and achievable steps that will help to achieve the goals. They should include a timeline for completion and a plan for monitoring and evaluating progress.

When developing an action plan, managers should first break down the goals into smaller, more manageable tasks. This will make the goals more achievable and will also make it easier to track progress. For example, if the goal is to increase sales, the action plan could include tasks such as conducting market research, launching a new product, or implementing a new marketing campaign.

Managers should also involve team members in the process of developing and implementing action plans. This will help to ensure that all team members understand the goals and their role in achieving them. It will also help to foster a sense of ownership and accountability among team members.

When implementing action plans, managers should also be prepared to make adjustments as needed. This could include changing the timeline, allocating more resources, or modifying the action plan to better reflect the organization's current situation.

Managers should also monitor and evaluate progress on a regular basis. This will help to ensure that the action plan is on track, and that any necessary adjustments can be made in a timely manner.

Developing and implementing action plans is a crucial step in achieving goals. Action plans should be specific, measurable, and achievable, include a timeline for completion and a plan for monitoring and evaluating progress. Managers should involve team members in the process, be prepared to make adjustments as needed, and monitor and evaluate progress regularly to ensure the action plan is on track. By doing so, managers can help to ensure that their teams are working towards the same objectives and that they are in line with the overall direction of the organization, which will ultimately lead to success.

Measuring and Evaluating Progress

Keeping track of success

Measuring and evaluating progress is an essential part of setting objectives and developing strategies. It allows managers to track progress towards achieving goals and make adjustments as needed. There are a variety of tools that managers can use to measure and evaluate progress, such as performance metrics, key performance indicators, and progress reports. Performance metrics are quantitative measures of the organization's performance, such as sales figures, customer satisfaction scores, or production numbers. Key performance indicators, or KPIs, are specific, measurable goals that are used to track progress towards achieving the organization's objectives. Progress reports provide detailed information on the progress made towards achieving goals.

Key performance indicators, or KPIs, are specific, measurable goals that are used to track progress towards achieving the organization's objectives. They provide a clear and quantifiable way to measure progress and are useful for tracking the performance of the organization, departments, and individual team members.

When selecting KPIs, managers should ensure that they align with the overall goals and objectives of the organization and are relevant to the specific department or team. They should also be specific, measurable, and achievable. For example, if the goal is to increase sales, a KPI could be the number of sales made per month or the percentage increase in sales compared to the previous year.

KPIs should be regularly monitored and reported on, with progress tracked over time. This can be done through regular progress reports or by using performance management software. Managers should use the information gathered to make adjustments as needed, such as allocating more resources, or modifying the action plan to better reflect the organization's current situation.

KPIs are also useful for setting individual goals for team members and providing regular feedback on performance. By setting individual KPIs and regularly monitoring progress, managers can help to ensure that team members are aligned with the overall goals and objectives of the organization, and can take corrective action if necessary.

Key performance indicators, or KPIs, are a useful tool for tracking progress towards achieving the organization's objectives. They provide a clear and quantifiable way to measure progress and are useful for tracking the performance of the organization, departments, and individual team members.

When selecting KPIs, managers should ensure that they align with the overall goals and objectives of the organization, are relevant to the specific department or team and are specific, measurable, and achievable. They should be regularly monitored and reported on, with progress tracked over time, used for setting individual goals for team members and providing regular feedback on performance.

Managers should also involve team members in the process of measuring and evaluating progress. This will help to ensure that all team members understand the goals and their role in achieving them, and it will also help to foster a sense of ownership and accountability among team members.

When evaluating progress, managers should also consider the impact of external factors, such as changes in the business environment or market conditions. This will help to ensure that progress is being evaluated in the context of the organization's overall situation.

Managers should also use the information gathered during the process of measuring and evaluating progress to make adjustments as needed. This could include changing the timeline, allocating more resources, or modifying the action plan to better reflect the organization's current situation. Measuring and evaluating progress is an essential part of setting objectives and developing strategies. It allows managers to track progress towards achieving goals and make adjustments as needed. Managers can use a variety of tools such as performance metrics, key performance indicators, and progress reports to measure and evaluate progress. Involving team members in the process and considering the impact of external factors, and using the information gathered to make adjustments as needed are important steps to ensure progress is being evaluated in the context of the organization's overall situation, which will ultimately lead to success.

Strategic Thinking

Anticipating and responding to change

Strategic thinking is an important aspect of setting objectives and developing strategies. It involves thinking about the long-term direction of the organization and considering how to adapt to changing circumstances. This can help managers to anticipate and respond to changes in the business environment and make decisions that will help to achieve success.

One effective approach to strategic thinking is to conduct a PESTLE analysis. PESTLE analysis is a tool that helps managers to identify and analyze the Political, Economic, Sociocultural, Technological, Environmental and Legal factors that may impact the organization. By understanding the external factors that can affect the organization, managers can anticipate and respond to changes in the business environment.

When conducting a PESTLE analysis, it is important to consider the following do's and don'ts:

Do's:

Do consider the political, economic, sociocultural, technological, environmental, and legal factors that may impact the organization.

Do analyze the factors in detail and consider how they may change in the future.

Do consider the impact of the factors on the organization as well as on the industry and market in which it operates.

Do use the information gathered to anticipate and respond to changes in the business environment.

Do consider the information gathered when making strategic decisions for the organization.

Don'ts:

Don't limit the analysis to only one or two factors, consider all of the factors that may impact the organization.

Don't only consider the current situation, anticipate how the factors may change in the future.

Don't ignore the external factors, they can have a significant impact on the organization.

Don't forget to consider the impact of the factors on different stakeholders such as customers, employees, shareholders and the community.

Don't use the information gathered only once, it should be regularly updated and considered when making decisions.

A PESTLE analysis is a useful tool for managers to anticipate and respond to changes in the business environment. It is important to consider all the factors that may impact the organization, analyze them in detail, consider the impact of the factors on the organization and the industry, use the information gathered to anticipate and respond to changes, and regularly update and consider the information when making decisions.

Another approach to strategic thinking is scenario planning. This involves creating multiple scenarios of how the organization may be impacted by different external factors and then identifying the actions that the organization should take to best respond to each scenario. This can help managers to be better prepared for a range of potential outcomes.

Managers should also be open to new ideas and perspectives. This can help to ensure that they are considering different options and making informed decisions. Managers should also encourage an open and creative culture within their teams, which will help to foster innovation and new ideas.

Finally, managers should be willing to take calculated risks. This means being willing to make a decision even when there is a degree of uncertainty, and being prepared to adapt to new situations as they arise.

Strategic thinking is an important aspect of setting objectives and developing strategies. It involves thinking about the long-term direction of the organization and considering how to adapt to changing circumstances. Managers can use tools such as PESTLE analysis and scenario planning to anticipate and respond to changes in the business environment. They should be open to new ideas and perspectives, encourage an open and creative culture within their teams, and be willing to take calculated risks. By doing so, managers can help to ensure that their teams are working towards the same objectives and that they are in line with the overall direction of the organization, which will ultimately lead to success.

Application

The principles and techniques discussed in the chapter on Setting Objectives and Developing Strategies can be applied in various ways in an organization. Here are a few examples of how they can be applied:

Managers can use SWOT analysis to identify and prioritize goals for the organization, departments, or teams. This can help to ensure that the goals are aligned with the overall direction of the organization and that resources are being allocated effectively.

Action plans can be developed and implemented by managers to achieve specific goals. This can help to ensure that team members understand their roles and responsibilities, and that progress is being made towards achieving the goals.

Measuring and evaluating progress can be used by managers to track progress towards achieving goals and make adjustments as needed. This can help to ensure that goals are being met and that the organization is on track to achieve its objectives.

Managers can use strategic thinking to anticipate and respond to changes in the business environment. This can help to ensure that the organization is well-positioned to adapt to new circumstances and that decisions are being made with the long-term direction of the organization in mind.

Managers can use PESTLE analysis and scenario planning to anticipate and respond to changes in the business environment. This can help to ensure that the organization is well-positioned to adapt to new circumstances and that decisions are being made with the long-term direction of the organization in mind.

Setting Objectives and Developing Strategies can be applied to identify and prioritize goals, develop, and implement action plans, measure, and evaluate progress, anticipate, and respond to changes in the business environment, and ensure that the organization is well-positioned to adapt to new circumstances and that decisions are being made with the long-term direction of the organization in mind.

Summary

In the chapter on Setting Objectives and Developing Strategies, we discussed a variety of tools and techniques that managers can use to achieve success. We covered the importance of setting specific, measurable, and achievable goals, developing, and implementing action plans, measuring, and evaluating progress, being open to new ideas and perspectives, and being willing to take calculated risks. We also discussed the importance of strategic thinking and utilizing tools such as PESTLE analysis and scenario planning to anticipate and respond to changes in the business environment. By applying these principles and techniques, managers can ensure that their teams are working towards the same objectives, that they are in line with the overall direction of the organization, and that they are well-positioned to adapt to new circumstances, which will ultimately lead to success.

CHAPTER 6

Making Decisions
and Solving Problems

Decision-making and problem-solving are critical skills for any manager. In this chapter, we will explore various techniques and approaches to making effective decisions and solving problems. We will discuss the importance of gathering and analyzing information, considering multiple options, and evaluating the potential outcomes of each option. We will also explore the role of creativity and innovation in decision-making and problem-solving, and provide strategies for dealing with uncertainty and risk. The goal of this chapter is to equip managers with the tools and knowledge needed to make effective decisions and solve problems in a timely and efficient manner.

Effective decision-making and problem-solving are essential for any manager, as they are central to the success of any organization. Whether it is making strategic decisions that will shape the direction of the organization, or solving day-to-day problems that arise within the team, managers are constantly faced with challenges that require them to make decisions and solve problems.

One key aspect of effective decision-making and problem-solving is the ability to gather and analyze information. This includes not only identifying the problem or decision that needs to be made, but also gathering relevant data and information that will inform the decision or solution. Managers must also be able to evaluate the potential outcomes of different options and consider the potential risks and benefits of each. Creativity and innovation are also important in decision-making and problem-solving. Managers should be open to new ideas and perspectives, and be willing to consider unconventional solutions. By fostering an open and creative culture within their teams, managers can encourage their team members to think outside the box and come up with innovative solutions.

Dealing with uncertainty and risk is another important aspect of decision-making and problem-solving. In many situations, managers will be required to make decisions with incomplete information or in uncertain circumstances. In these cases, it is important for managers to be able to assess the potential risks and make informed decisions based on the information available.

Decision-making and problem-solving are critical skills for any manager, as they are central to the success of any organization. In this chapter we will explore various techniques and approaches to making effective decisions and solving problems. This includes gathering and analyzing information, considering multiple options, evaluating the potential outcomes of each option, fostering creativity and innovation, and dealing with uncertainty and risk. The goal of this chapter is to equip managers with the tools and knowledge needed to make effective decisions and solve problems in a timely and efficient manner.

Gather and Analyze Information

The foundation of effective decision-making and problem-solving

The first step in making effective decisions and solving problems is to gather and analyze information. This includes not only identifying the problem or decision that needs to be made, but also gathering relevant data and information that will inform the decision or solution. Managers must be able to evaluate the potential outcomes of different options and consider the potential risks and benefits of each.

One effective approach to gathering and analyzing information is to conduct a root cause analysis. This involves identifying the underlying causes of a problem, rather than just treating the symptoms. By identifying the root cause of a problem, managers can develop a more effective solution that addresses the underlying issue.

Another approach is to use a decision matrix. A decision matrix is a tool that helps managers to evaluate different options by considering a set of criteria. This can help managers to make informed decisions by comparing the potential outcomes of different options against a set of established criteria.

Managers must also be able to evaluate the potential outcomes of different options and consider the potential risks and benefits of each. This can be done by creating a risk management plan. A risk management plan is a tool that helps managers to identify, assess and manage the risks associated with a particular decision or course of action.Gather and Analyze Information is a key aspect of effective decision-making and problem-solving. It includes identifying the problem or decision that needs to be made, gathering relevant data and information that will inform the decision or solution, evaluating the potential outcomes of different options, considering the potential risks and benefits of each, and using tools such as root cause analysis, decision matrix and risk management plan to inform the decision or solution. By gathering and analyzing information, managers can ensure that they have the necessary information to make informed decisions and solve problems effectively.

The process of gathering and analyzing information can be broken down into several steps:

1. Identify the problem or decision that needs to be made. Clearly define the issue or question that needs to be addressed.

2. Gather relevant data and information. Collect data from various sources such as reports, surveys, interviews, and observations. It's important to consider multiple perspectives and to validate the information gathered.

3. Evaluate the potential outcomes of different options. Analyze the information gathered, identify the potential solutions, and compare the potential outcomes of each option against the identified criteria.

4. Consider the potential risks and benefits of each option. Identify potential risks associated with each option and weigh them against the potential benefits.

5. Use tools such as root cause analysis, decision matrix and risk management plan to inform the decision or solution. Apply these tools to the information gathered to help inform the decision or solution in a more structured and analytical way.

6. Make a decision or implement the chosen solution. After evaluating the potential outcomes, risks and benefits of each option, select the option that best aligns with the organization's goals, values and objectives.

When gathering and analyzing information, it is important to consider the following do's and don'ts:

Do's:

Do identify the problem or decision that needs to be made.

Do gather relevant data and information that will inform the decision or solution.

Do evaluate the potential outcomes of different options.

Do consider the potential risks and benefits of each option.

Do use tools such as root cause analysis, decision matrix and risk management plan to inform the decision or solution.

Don'ts:

Don't limit the information gathering to only one or two sources, gather information from multiple sources to ensure a well-rounded view.

Don't ignore or discard information that contradicts your initial beliefs or assumptions, consider all information and be open to new perspectives.

Don't only consider short-term outcomes, also consider long-term effects and consequences of the decision or solution.

Don't make assumptions about the information, verify and validate the information before using it to inform the decision or solution.

Don't ignore or postpone gathering and analyzing information, it is important to have the necessary information to make informed decisions and solve problems effectively.

Gathering and Analyzing information is a process that involves identifying the problem or decision that needs to be made, gathering relevant data and information, evaluating the potential outcomes of different options, considering the potential risks and benefits of each option, using tools such as root cause analysis, decision matrix and risk management plan to inform the decision or solution, and finally making a decision or implementing the chosen solution. By following these steps, managers can ensure that they have the necessary information to make informed decisions and solve problems effectively.

Creativity and Innovation

Breaking out of the box to find new solutions

Creativity and innovation are essential for effective decision-making and problem-solving, as they can lead to new and unconventional solutions. Managers should be open to new ideas and perspectives, and be willing to consider unconventional solutions. By fostering an open and creative culture within their teams, managers can encourage their team members to think outside the box and come up with innovative solutions.

One effective approach to fostering creativity and innovation is to promote a culture of experimentation and learning. This can be done by encouraging team members to try new things and to learn from their mistakes. By creating an environment where team members feel comfortable taking risks and experimenting, managers can foster creativity and innovation.

Another approach is to use brainstorming and idea generation techniques. Brainstorming is a method of generating ideas by encouraging team members to share their thoughts and ideas freely without fear of criticism. Idea generation techniques such as SCAMPER, which is an acronym for Substitute, Combine, Adapt, Modify, Put to another use,

Eliminate, Reverse, can also be used to encourage team members to think outside the box and come up with new ideas.

SCAMPER is a technique used to generate new ideas and solutions by encouraging creativity and thinking outside the box. The SCAMPER technique can be used to analyze a product, service, or process, and to identify opportunities for improvement or innovation.

Here are five ways to use the SCAMPER technique:

Substitute: This step involves looking at different elements of a product, service, or process, and identifying ways to replace them with something else. For example, in the case of a product, one could substitute a component with a cheaper or more efficient alternative.

Combine: This step involves looking at ways to combine different elements of a product, service, or process, to create something new. For example, in the case of a product, one could combine two or more features to create a new product.

Adapt: This step involves looking at ways to adapt a product, service or process to a new market, audience, or application. For example, a product designed for one market could be adapted for another market.

Modify: This step involves looking at ways to make changes or improvements to an existing product, service, or process. For example, in the case of a product, one could modify its design, size or color.

Put to another use: This step involves looking at ways to use an existing product, service, or process in a new way. For example, one could use a product for a new application or for a new market.

Eliminate: This step involves looking at ways to eliminate unnecessary elements of a product, service, or process. For example, in the case of a product, one could eliminate a component that is not essential to its function.

Reverse: This step involves looking at a product, service, or process from a different perspective, and reversing its elements. For example, in the case of a product, one could reverse its function, or use it in an opposite way.

When used properly, SCAMPER can aid in generating new ideas and solutions by encouraging creativity and thinking outside the box. It can be used to analyze a product, service, or process and to identify opportunities for improvement or innovation. By following these steps, managers can encourage their team members to think outside the box and come up with innovative solutions.

Managers can also encourage creativity and innovation by providing opportunities for team members to work on projects outside of their usual role or expertise. By allowing team members to work on projects that are outside of their comfort zone, managers can expose them to new perspectives and ideas, and can foster creativity and innovation.

Creativity and Innovation are important for effective decision-making and problem-solving. Managers should be open to new ideas and perspectives, and be willing to consider unconventional solutions. By fostering an open and creative culture within their teams, promoting experimentation and learning, using brainstorming and idea generation techniques, and providing opportunities for team members to work on projects outside of their usual role or expertise, managers can encourage their team members to think outside the box and come up with innovative solutions.

Managing Uncertainty and Risk

Navigating the unknown in decision-making and problem-solving

Uncertainty and risk are inherent in decision-making and problem-solving. Managers must be able to navigate the unknown and make decisions in the face of uncertainty and risk. By proactively identifying and managing uncertainty and risk, managers can minimize the potential negative impact and capitalize on potential opportunities.

One approach to managing uncertainty and risk is to use scenario planning. Scenario planning involves creating different potential scenarios and then developing a plan for each scenario. This can help managers to anticipate potential challenges and opportunities, and to be prepared to respond if they occur.

Scenario planning is a tool that can be used to help managers anticipate potential challenges and opportunities, and to be prepared to respond if they occur. It is a process of creating different potential scenarios and then developing a plan for each scenario. Here are five key elements of scenario planning:

Identify key drivers: Scenario planning starts with identifying the key drivers that are likely to shape the future. These drivers could be economic, political, technological, or environmental factors, among others.

Create a set of scenarios: Once the key drivers have been identified, the next step is to create a set of scenarios that reflect different combinations of these drivers. These scenarios should be plausible, but not necessarily probable.

Assess the implications of each scenario: Once the scenarios have been created, the next step is to assess the implications of each scenario. This includes identifying the potential impact on the organization, its stakeholders, and its environment.

Develop plans for each scenario: The final step is to develop plans for each scenario. These plans should be flexible and adaptable, and should consider both short-term and long-term implications.

Continuously monitor and update: Scenario planning is not a one-time exercise, it should be continuously monitored and updated as the situation evolves. By continuously monitoring and updating the scenarios, managers can adjust their plans as needed and stay prepared for any potential challenges and opportunities.

Scenario planning is a process of creating different potential scenarios and then developing a plan for each scenario. It starts with identifying the key drivers that are likely to shape the future, creating a set of scenarios that reflect different combinations of these drivers, assessing the implications of each scenario, developing plans for each scenario, and continuously monitoring and updating it as the situation evolves. By using scenario planning, managers can anticipate potential challenges and opportunities, and be prepared to respond if they occur.

Another approach is to use a decision tree. A decision tree is a tool that helps managers to evaluate different options by considering the potential outcomes and risks associated with each option. By using a decision tree, managers can identify the most favorable option based on the potential outcomes and risks.

A decision tree is a tool that helps managers to evaluate different options by considering the potential outcomes and risks associated with each option. It is a visual representation of the decision-making process that shows the potential outcomes of each option and the probabilities of those outcomes.

Here are five key elements of using a decision tree:

Identify the decision or problem: The first step in using a decision tree is to clearly identify the decision or problem that needs to be addressed.

Identify the options: Once the decision or problem has been identified, the next step is to identify the options that are available. These options should be mutually exclusive and collectively exhaustive.

Assess the potential outcomes: The next step is to assess the potential outcomes of each option. This includes identifying the potential benefits and costs, as well as the likelihood of each outcome.

Evaluate the options: The next step is to evaluate the options by considering the potential outcomes and the likelihood of each outcome. This can be done by calculating the expected value of each option.

Make a decision: After evaluating the options, the final step is to make a decision. The option with the highest expected value is typically considered the best option. However, other factors such as risk tolerance and constraints should also be considered in the decision- making process.

A decision tree is a tool that helps managers to evaluate different options by considering the potential outcomes and risks associated with each option. It is a visual representation of the decision-making process that shows the potential outcomes of each option and the probabilities of those outcomes. By following these five steps, managers can use a decision tree to make informed decisions and to navigate uncertainty and risk.

Managers can also use sensitivity analysis to identify the factors that have the greatest impact on the potential outcomes of a decision. Sensitivity analysis helps managers to identify the areas where a small change can result in a large impact, and to focus their attention on those areas.

Sensitivity analysis is a tool that can be used to identify the factors that have the greatest impact on the potential outcomes of a decision. It is a process of evaluating how a change in one or more variables will affect the outcome of a decision.

Here are five key elements of sensitivity analysis:

Identify the key variables: The first step in sensitivity analysis is to identify the key variables that are likely to have an impact on the decision. These variables could be costs, revenues, market conditions, or other factors.

Assess the impact of each variable: Once the key variables have been identified, the next step is to assess the impact of each variable on the decision. This includes identifying the potential impact of each variable on the outcome of the decision.

Determine the range of each variable: The next step is to determine the range of each variable. This includes identifying the minimum and maximum values for each variable and the likelihood of each value within that range.

Evaluate the sensitivity of the decision: The next step is to evaluate the sensitivity of the decision by simulating different combinations of variables and assessing the impact on the outcome.

Identify the critical variables: The final step is to identify the critical variables, which are the variables that have the greatest impact on the outcome of the decision. By focusing on these critical variables, managers can make more informed decisions and minimize the impact of uncertainty.

Sensitivity analysis is a tool that can be used to identify the factors that have the greatest impact on the potential outcomes of a decision. It is a process of evaluating how a change in one or more variables will affect the outcome of a decision. By following these five steps, managers can use sensitivity analysis to identify the critical variables that have the greatest impact on the outcome of the decision, and make more informed decisions and minimize the impact of uncertainty.

Managers can also use Monte Carlo simulation to evaluate the potential outcomes of a decision under different conditions. Monte Carlo simulation can help managers to identify the potential range of outcomes and the probability of each outcome, which can be useful in decision-making.

Monte Carlo simulation is a tool that can be used to evaluate the potential outcomes of a decision under different conditions. It is a mathematical technique that uses random sampling to simulate the behavior of a system.

Here are five key elements of using Monte Carlo simulation:

Identify the problem: The first step in using Monte Carlo simulation is to clearly identify the problem or decision that needs to be addressed.

Define the model: The next step is to define the model. This includes identifying the variables that are likely to affect the outcome of the decision, and the relationships between these variables.

Generate random values: The next step is to generate random values for the variables in the model. These values should be consistent with the probability distributions of the variables.

Run the simulation: The next step is to run the simulation by plugging in the random values into the model and evaluating the outcome. This should be repeated a large number of times to produce a distribution of outcomes.

Analyze the results: The final step is to analyze the results of the simulation. This includes identifying the most likely outcome, as well as the range of possible outcomes and their probabilities.

The Monte Carlo simulation is a tool that can be used to evaluate the potential outcomes of a decision under different conditions. It is a mathematical technique that uses random sampling to simulate the behavior of a system. By following these five steps, managers can use Monte Carlo simulation to identify the potential range of outcomes and the probability of each outcome, which can be useful in decision-making. This can help managers to make more informed decisions by considering the potential range of outcomes and the probability of each outcome.

Application

Making decisions and solving problems are essential responsibilities of managers. By using a combination of tools such as Gather and Analyze Information, SCAMPER, Decision tree, Sensitivity analysis, and Monte Carlo simulation, managers can make informed decisions and navigate uncertainty and risk.

In real-world applications, a manager might use Gather and Analyze Information to research and evaluate different options for a new product launch. They might use SCAMPER to generate new ideas and improve an existing product. They might use a Decision tree to evaluate the potential outcomes and risks of different marketing strategies. They might use Sensitivity analysis to identify the critical variables that will have the greatest impact on the success of the product launch. Finally, they might use Monte Carlo simulation to evaluate the potential outcomes of different budget scenarios.

In terms of problem-solving, a manager might use Gather and Analyze Information to research and understand the root cause of a problem within their organization. They might use SCAMPER to generate new solutions to the problem. They might use a Decision tree to evaluate the potential outcomes and risks of different solutions. They might use Sensitivity analysis to identify the critical variables that will have the greatest impact on the success of the solution.

Finally, they might use Monte Carlo simulation to evaluate the potential outcomes of different solutions under different scenarios.

The techniques and tools discussed in the chapter "Making Decisions and Solving Problems" can be applied in various ways depending on the problem or decision at hand. By applying these techniques and tools, managers can make better decisions and solve problems more effectively.

Summary

In summary, Managing Uncertainty and Risk is an important aspect of decision-making and problem-solving. By proactively identifying and managing uncertainty and risk, managers can minimize the potential negative impact and capitalize on potential opportunities. By using tools such as scenario planning, decision tree, sensitivity analysis, and Monte Carlo simulation, managers can navigate the unknown and make decisions effectively.

CHAPTER 7

Managing Time
and Prioritizing Tasks

Managing time and prioritizing tasks are essential skills for any manager. With the fast-paced nature of today's business world, it is more important than ever to be able to effectively manage one's time and prioritize tasks in order to achieve goals and meet deadlines. This chapter will explore the importance of time management and prioritization and provide strategies and techniques for improving these skills. We will examine different time management tools and methods, as well as ways to prioritize tasks and manage competing demands. By the end of this chapter, readers will have a better understanding of how to manage their time and prioritize tasks effectively, in order to achieve their goals and be more productive.

Effective time management and task prioritization are essential skills for managers, as they allow them to be more productive and achieve their goals. By managing their time effectively, managers can ensure that they are using their time in the most efficient way possible, and that they are able to complete the tasks that are most important to their organization. Prioritizing tasks is also important, as it allows managers to focus on the most important tasks and avoid wasting time on less important tasks. Additionally, managing time and prioritizing tasks can help managers to be more effective in their roles, as they are able to complete tasks on time and meet deadlines.

Understanding Time Management Techniques and Tools

Understanding Time Management Techniques and Tools: Time management techniques and tools can help managers to be more productive and achieve their goals. One popular technique is the Pomodoro Technique, which involves breaking work into 25-minute intervals, followed by a five-minute break. This technique helps to increase focus and reduce fatigue. Another popular tool is the Eisenhower matrix, which helps managers to prioritize tasks by dividing them into four categories: urgent and important, important but not urgent, urgent but not important, and not important or urgent. By using these techniques and tools, managers can better understand how they are using their time and make changes to be more productive.

DO's for the Pomodoro Technique:

Define the task: Before starting a Pomodoro, make sure you have a clear understanding of what you need to accomplish. Break down larger tasks into smaller, more manageable chunks.

Set a timer: Use a timer to keep track of your 25-minute work intervals and 5-minute breaks.

Work in uninterrupted chunks: During the 25-minute work intervals, focus on the task at hand and avoid distractions.

Take short breaks: Take a 5-minute break after each 25-minute work interval. Use this time to stretch, relax, or do something enjoyable.

Use a to-do list: Keep a to-do list to keep track of your tasks and monitor your progress.

Take a longer break after 4 Pomodoro: After four 25-minute work intervals, take a longer break of 15-20 minutes to recharge.

DON'Ts for the Pomodoro Technique:

Don't multitask: The Pomodoro Technique is designed to help you focus on one task at a time.

Avoid multitasking during the 25-minute work intervals.

Don't skip the breaks: It is important to take the 5-minute breaks to rest and recharge your brain. Skipping breaks can lead to burnout and decreased productivity.

Don't let interruptions disrupt your work: Try to minimize interruptions during the 25-minute work intervals. If you can't avoid them, make sure to note the time and return to the task after the interruption.

Don't overwork: Remember to take a longer break after 4 Pomodoros and don't overwork yourself. Overworking can lead to burnout and decreased productivity.

Don't be too strict: The Pomodoro Technique is a flexible tool, don't be too strict with it and adapt it to your needs.

Don't use it for all tasks: Some tasks may require longer periods of focus, or may not be suitable for the Pomodoro Technique, feel free to adjust the time intervals or not use it at all for some tasks.

Another technique is the "ABCDE" method, which stands for "Must do, Should do, Could do, Would like to do, and Won't do." This method allows managers to prioritize their tasks by sorting them into different categories based on their importance. Tasks in the "A" category are the most important and must be done immediately, while tasks in the "B" category are important but can be done later. Tasks in the "C" category are less important and can be delegated or deferred, and tasks in the "D" and "E" categories are non-essential and can be eliminated.

DO's for the "ABCDE" method:

Sort tasks into categories: Sort your tasks into the different categories, A, B, C, D, and E, based on their importance and urgency.

Tackle A tasks first: Focus on completing tasks in the A category first, as they are the most important and urgent.

Don't procrastinate B tasks: B tasks are important but not urgent, don't procrastinate them as they are still important and have to be done.

Delegate or defer C tasks: C tasks are less important and can be delegated to others or deferred to a later time.

Eliminate D and E tasks: D and E tasks are non-essential and can be eliminated if possible.

Review and adjust: Review your task list regularly and adjust your priorities as needed.

DON'Ts for the "ABCDE" method:

Don't mix up the categories: Be consistent in sorting your tasks into the different categories, and don't mix them up.

Don't neglect B tasks: B tasks are important and should not be neglected, they have to be done.

Don't delegate or defer A tasks: A tasks are the most important and should be tackled first, don't delegate or defer them.

Don't do D and E tasks: D and E tasks are non-essential and should be eliminated if possible.

Don't procrastinate: Don't put off completing tasks, prioritize them and tackle them as soon as possible.

Don't overburden yourself: Don't take on too many tasks, prioritize them and manage your workload according to your capacity. The "80/20" rule, also known as Pareto's principle, states that 80% of results come from 20% of efforts. This principle can be used to identify the most important tasks and focus on them. By identifying the tasks that will have the greatest impact on achieving goals, managers can prioritize them and allocate their time and resources accordingly.

DO's for the 80/20 rule:

Identify the most important tasks: Use the 80/20 rule to identify the tasks that will have the greatest impact on achieving your goals.

Prioritize these tasks: Prioritize the most important tasks and allocate your time and resources accordingly.

Focus on the highest-yielding activities: Focus on the activities that will yield the greatest results and have the greatest impact on your goals.

Delegate or outsource: Delegate or outsource tasks that are less important or that someone else can do more efficiently.

Measure your results: Measure your results to determine the effectiveness of your efforts and make adjustments as needed.

Be flexible: Be flexible and adjust your priorities as necessary to make the best use of your time and resources.

DON'Ts for the 80/20 rule:

Don't neglect low-yielding activities: Don't neglect low-yielding activities entirely, as they may still be important and need to be done.

Don't overlook the importance of less critical tasks: Some less critical tasks may still be important for the overall success of your goals and should not be ignored.

Don't over-delegate: Don't over-delegate tasks, as delegating too much can lead to loss of control and quality.

Don't forget to measure: Don't forget to measure the results of your efforts to see if you are on the right track.

Don't become too rigid: Don't become too rigid in sticking to the 80/20 rule and forget to adjust your priorities as needed.

Don't forget that the 80/20 rule is just a rule of thumb, it may not always apply in every situation, so use it as a general guide but adjust it as needed.

Setting SMART goals is another important aspect of effective time management. SMART goals are Specific, Measurable, Achievable, Relevant, and Time-bound. By setting SMART goals, manager can ensure that they are working towards specific and measurable objectives, and they can track their progress and make adjustments as needed.

DO's for SMART goals:

Make sure your goals are Specific: Be clear and specific about what you want to accomplish and what you need to do to achieve it.

Make sure your goals are Measurable: Set measurable goals so you can track your progress and know when you've achieved them.

Make sure your goals are Achievable: Set realistic and achievable goals that you can accomplish given the resources and constraints.

Make sure your goals are Relevant: Make sure your goals align with your overall objectives and are relevant to your current situation.

Make sure your goals are Time-bound: Set a deadline for achieving your goals so you can stay motivated and focused.

Write your goals down: Writing your goals down helps you to clarify your thoughts, makes them more concrete and increases the chances of achieving them.

Review your goals regularly: Review your goals regularly to stay on track and make adjustments as needed.

DON'Ts for SMART goals:

Don't set goals that are not Specific: Avoid setting goals that are too general or vague, as they are less likely to be achieved.

Don't set goals that are not Measurable: Avoid setting goals that can't be measured, as you will not be able to track your progress or know when you've achieved them.

Don't set goals that are not Achievable: Avoid setting goals that are unrealistic or impossible to achieve, as they can lead to frustration and disappointment.

Don't set goals that are not Relevant: Avoid setting goals that are not relevant to your overall objectives or current situation, as they may not be worth pursuing.

Don't set goals without a deadline: Avoid setting goals without a deadline, as they can be easily put off and forgotten.

Don't set too many goals at once: Avoid setting too many goals at once as it can be overwhelming, focus on a few important ones at a time.

Don't be too rigid: Don't be too rigid in sticking to your goals and forget to adjust them as needed. Time blocking is another effective technique that managers can use to manage their time. Time blocking involves scheduling specific blocks of time for specific tasks. This helps to reduce distractions, increase focus and productivity, and ensure that important tasks are completed.

DO's for Time Blocking:

Define your priorities: Determine what tasks are most important and should be given priority in your schedule.

Block out time for specific tasks: Set aside specific blocks of time for individual tasks or activities, and stick to them as closely as possible.

Use a calendar or planner: Use a calendar or planner to schedule your time blocks and keep track of your schedule.

Be realistic: Be realistic about how much time you need for each task, and adjust your schedule accordingly.

Include breaks: Make sure to include breaks in your schedule to rest and recharge.

Be flexible: Be flexible and adjust your schedule as needed, taking into account unexpected events or changes in priorities.

Allow some buffer time: Allow some buffer time in between tasks or activities to make sure you don't fall behind schedule.

DON'Ts for Time Blocking:

Don't overschedule: Avoid scheduling more activities than you can realistically handle, as this can lead to burnout and stress.

Don't neglect self-care: Don't neglect self-care and rest in your schedule, as it is important for productivity and well-being.

Don't neglect other important responsibilities: Don't neglect other important responsibilities, such as family, friends, or personal development, in favor of work or other activities.

Don't forget to be flexible: Don't forget to be flexible and adjust your schedule as needed.

Don't block out too much time for one task: Don't block out too much time for one task, as this can lead to procrastination and a lack of focus.

Don't forget to review and adjust your schedule regularly: Don't forget to review and adjust your schedule regularly to make sure it still aligns with your priorities and goals.

Don't be too rigid: Don't be too rigid in following your schedule and forget to allow some flexibility. There are a variety of time management techniques and tools that managers can use to be more productive and achieve their goals. These include the Pomodoro Technique, Eisenhower matrix, ABCDE method, 80/20 rule, SMART goals, and Time blocking. By understanding these techniques and tools and using them effectively, managers can better manage their time and prioritize tasks, which can lead to increased productivity and efficiency.

Prioritizing Tasks and Managing Demands

Prioritizing tasks and managing demands is a critical skill for any manager, as it allows them to effectively utilize their time and resources to achieve goals. One key strategy for prioritizing tasks is to use a task matrix, which allows managers to categorize tasks based on their importance and urgency.

A task matrix, also known as a task prioritization matrix, is a simple tool used to prioritize tasks based on their importance and urgency. The matrix typically consists of a grid or table with four quadrants, each representing a different level of priority.

The quadrants are typically labeled as:

High importance, high urgency: These tasks are considered top priority and must be completed immediately. They typically include tasks that have a strict deadline, are critical for the success of the project or are legally mandated.

High importance, low urgency: These tasks are also considered important but can be completed at a later time. They are typically long-term projects or strategic initiatives that are important for the organization's success.

Low importance, high urgency: These tasks are considered less important but must be completed soon. They may include administrative tasks or routine maintenance that need to be done but do not have a direct impact on the success of the project or organization.

Low importance, low urgency: These tasks are considered least important and can be deferred or delegated. They may include tasks that are not directly related to the project or organization's goals and can be completed at a later time.

By categorizing tasks into these four quadrants, managers can quickly identify which tasks are most important and should be given priority, and which tasks can be deferred or delegated. This can help managers to effectively utilize their time and resources to achieve their goals.

Another effective strategy is to use the Eisenhower matrix, which helps managers to identify the most important tasks and to distinguish between those that are urgent and those that are not.

The Eisenhower matrix, also known as the Eisenhower Decision Principle or Eisenhower Box, is a tool used to help prioritize tasks based on their urgency and importance. The matrix consists of four quadrants, each representing a different level of priority.

The quadrants are typically labeled as:

Urgent and important: These tasks are considered top priority and must be done immediately. They typically include tasks that have a strict deadline, are critical for the success of the project or are legally mandated.

Important but not urgent: These tasks are also considered important but can be completed at a later time. They are typically long-term projects or strategic initiatives that are important for the organization's success.

Urgent but not important: These tasks are considered less important but must be completed soon. They may include administrative tasks or routine maintenance that need to be done but do not have a direct impact on the success of the project or organization.

Not urgent and not important: These tasks are considered least important and can be deferred or delegated. They may include tasks that are not directly related to the project or organization's goals and can be completed at a later time.

The Eisenhower matrix can help managers to effectively prioritize their tasks by identifying which tasks are urgent and important and should be given priority, and which tasks are less important and can be deferred or delegated. It is a simple yet powerful tool that can help managers to stay organized and to achieve their goals efficiently.

It is also important for managers to learn how to say no and to set clear boundaries. This helps to manage expectations and to prevent taking on more tasks than can be reasonably accomplished.

Another important aspect of managing demands is to learn how to delegate effectively. By assigning tasks to other team members, managers can free up their own time and focus on more important tasks.

Finally, it is important for managers to stay organized and to use tools such as calendars, task lists, and project management software to help keep track of tasks and deadlines. By effectively prioritizing tasks and managing demands, managers can stay on top of their workload and achieve their goals.

Managing Meetings and Communication

Meetings and communication are an important part of any manager's role, but they can also be time-consuming and disruptive to workflow. To manage meetings and communication effectively, it's important to set clear agendas and objectives for each meeting, and to stick to a strict time limit.

Another effective strategy is to limit the number of meetings and only schedule them when they are truly necessary. This helps to reduce the number of interruptions and distractions, and allows you to focus on other important tasks.

When it comes to communication, it's important to use the most efficient means possible. For example, instead of scheduling a meeting, consider using email or instant messaging for quick updates or simple questions.

Additionally, it is important to be mindful of the frequency and content of communication, as over-communication can lead to a cluttered inbox and wasted time.

Finally, it is also important to actively listen and be responsive to the needs and concerns of team members, stakeholders, and colleagues. By fostering open and effective communication, managers can build trust and create a more productive and positive work environment.

Managing priorities and delegation are crucial skills for any manager, as they are essential for effectively utilizing the resources of a team and accomplishing goals. One way to manage priorities is to create a task list or to-do list, and to prioritize tasks based on their importance and urgency.

Another way to manage priorities is to use a prioritization matrix. This is a tool that helps to identify which tasks are most important and should be given priority. It also helps to distinguish between high-priority tasks that must be done immediately and lower-priority tasks that can be deferred or delegated.

Delegation is another important aspect of managing priorities. It is the process of assigning tasks and responsibilities to others. By delegating effectively, managers can free up time for more important tasks and can also help to develop the skills and abilities of team members.

When delegating, it is important to choose the right person for the task, to provide clear instructions and expectations, and to provide support and guidance as needed.

Finally, it is also important to be mindful of the workload of team members and to avoid overloading them with too many tasks. By managing priorities and delegation effectively, managers can ensure that tasks are completed efficiently and that the team is working towards common goals.

Maximizing Productivity and Efficiency

Maximizing productivity and efficiency is essential for any manager, as it helps to ensure that goals are met and that resources are being used effectively. One key strategy for maximizing productivity is to set clear and measurable goals, and to track progress towards those goals. This can help managers to stay focused on what is important and to identify areas where improvements can be made.

Setting clear and measurable goals is an essential step in maximizing productivity and achieving success as a manager. One way to set clear and measurable goals is to use the SMART criteria, which stands for Specific, Measurable, Achievable, Relevant and Time-bound. This ensures that goals are well defined, quantifiable and have a clear deadline.

Another key aspect of setting clear and measurable goals is to ensure that they align with the overall vision and mission of the organization. This helps to ensure that goals are aligned with the organization's strategy and that they contribute to the overall success of the organization.

When setting goals, it's also important to involve team members and stakeholders, as this helps to ensure that everyone is working towards a common goal, and that the goals are achievable.

Another important aspect of setting clear and measurable goals is to break them down into smaller, manageable tasks. This allows managers to focus on one task at a time, and make progress towards the larger goal.

It is important to track progress and measure results. This helps managers to identify areas where improvements can be made, and to adjust goals as needed. By setting clear and measurable goals, managers can stay focused, achieve success, and maximize productivity.

Another effective strategy for maximizing productivity is to use time management techniques such as the Pomodoro Technique or time blocking. These techniques can help managers to stay organized and to break down large tasks into smaller, manageable chunks, making them easier to complete.

A third strategy for maximizing productivity is to minimize distractions and interruptions. This can be done by setting clear boundaries, such as setting specific times for checking email or limiting the number of meetings.

Another important aspect of maximizing productivity and efficiency is to create a positive and supportive work environment. This can be done by fostering collaboration and communication, and by providing team members with the resources and support they need to be successful.

It is also important for managers to stay up-to-date with the latest tools and technologies, as they can help to automate tasks, streamline workflows and make work more efficient. By implementing these strategies, managers can maximize productivity and efficiency, and achieve their goals more effectively.

Prioritizing tasks and maximizing productivity and efficiency is essential for any manager, as it allows them to effectively utilize their time and resources to achieve goals. One key strategy for prioritizing tasks is to use a task matrix, which allows managers to categorize tasks based on their importance and urgency. This helps to identify which tasks are most important and should be given priority, and which tasks can be deferred or delegated.

Another effective strategy for maximizing productivity is to use time management techniques such as the Pomodoro Technique or time blocking. These techniques can help managers to stay organized and to break down large tasks into smaller, manageable chunks, making them easier to complete.

Minimizing distractions and interruptions is also crucial in maximizing productivity and efficiency. This can be done by setting clear boundaries, such as setting specific times for checking email or limiting the number of meetings.

Another important aspect of maximizing productivity and efficiency is to create a positive and supportive work environment. This can be done by fostering collaboration and communication, and by providing team members with the resources and support they need to be successful.

Finally, it is also important to stay up-to-date with the latest tools and technologies, as they can help to automate tasks, streamline workflows and make work more efficient. By prioritizing tasks, implementing time management techniques, minimizing distractions, creating a positive work environment, and staying up-to-date with technology, managers can maximize productivity and efficiency, and achieve their goals more effectively.

Overcoming Procrastination and Distractions

Overcoming procrastination and distractions is a common challenge for many managers, as it can impede their ability to achieve goals and maximize productivity. One effective strategy for overcoming procrastination is to set clear and measurable goals, and to track progress towards those goals. This helps to keep managers focused on what is important and to identify areas where improvements can be made.

Another strategy for overcoming procrastination is to break down large tasks into smaller, manageable chunks. This makes tasks more manageable and less intimidating, making it easier to get started on them.

Minimizing distractions is also crucial in overcoming procrastination. This can be done by setting clear boundaries, such as limiting the number of meetings or setting specific times for checking email.

Another effective strategy for overcoming procrastination is to use time management techniques such as the Pomodoro Technique or time blocking. These techniques help managers to stay organized and to focus on specific tasks for a set period of time, making it easier to get started on them.

Finally, it's also important to identify and address the underlying causes of procrastination, such as lack of motivation or fear of failure. By identifying the root causes, managers can address them directly, and develop strategies to overcome them.

Overcoming procrastination and distractions is crucial for managers to achieve their goals, maximize productivity and efficiency, setting clear and measurable goals, breaking down tasks into manageable chunks, minimizing distractions, using time management techniques, and identifying and addressing underlying causes of procrastination can help managers overcome these challenges.

Application

Effective time management and task prioritization are essential skills for achieving success in both personal and professional settings. With the increasing demands of modern life, it can be challenging to balance multiple responsibilities and commitments while staying focused and productive. Fortunately, there are a variety of applications and techniques that can help individuals manage their time and prioritize tasks more effectively, allowing them to achieve their goals and improve their overall quality of life. In this section, we will review several applications and techniques for managing time and prioritizing tasks, and how they can be applied to increase productivity and achieve success.

To-Do List Apps: Using a to-do list app can be an effective way to manage time and prioritize tasks. These apps allow users to create a list of tasks, set deadlines, and prioritize tasks based on their importance and urgency. Many to-do list apps also offer features such as reminders, task notes, and the ability to categorize tasks, which can help users stay organized and on track.

Pomodoro Technique: The Pomodoro Technique is a time management method that involves breaking work into focused, 25-minute intervals (called pomodoros), followed by a short break. This technique can be useful for managing time and prioritizing tasks, as it encourages users to work in short bursts of focused activity and take breaks in between to recharge.

Time Tracking Software: Time tracking software can be an effective tool for managing time and prioritizing tasks, as it allows users to track how much time they spend on different tasks and activities throughout the day. This can help users identify areas where they are spending too much time, and prioritize tasks more effectively based on their importance and urgency.

Eisenhower Matrix: The Eisenhower Matrix is a prioritization tool that helps users sort tasks into four categories based on their importance and urgency: important and urgent, important but not urgent, urgent but not important, and neither important nor urgent. This can be a useful tool for managing time and prioritizing tasks, as it allows users to focus on the most important and urgent tasks first, while also making time for tasks that are important but not necessarily urgent.

Time Blocking: Time blocking involves scheduling blocks of time for specific tasks and activities throughout the day. This can be an effective way to manage time and prioritize tasks, as it helps users to stay focused and avoid distractions, while also making time for important tasks that might otherwise get overlooked.

By using these applications and techniques, individuals can effectively manage their time and prioritize tasks, which can lead to increased productivity, better time management, and a greater sense of control and accomplishment in their work.

Summary

Managing time and prioritizing tasks are crucial skills for individuals to achieve their goals and succeed in their personal and professional lives. To manage their time effectively, individuals can use applications and techniques such as to-do list apps, the Pomodoro Technique, time tracking software, the Eisenhower Matrix, and time blocking. These tools can help individuals to prioritize their tasks, organize their schedules, and stay focused and productive.

Using a to-do list app is a simple yet effective way to manage time and prioritize tasks. These apps allow users to create lists of tasks, set deadlines, and prioritize tasks based on their importance and urgency. The apps also offer features such as reminders, task notes, and the ability to categorize tasks, which can help users stay organized and on track.

The Pomodoro Technique is another technique that can help individuals manage their time effectively. This technique involves breaking work into focused, 25-minute intervals, followed by a short break. This can be useful for managing time and prioritizing tasks, as it encourages users to work in short bursts of focused activity and take breaks in between to recharge. Additionally, time tracking software and the Eisenhower Matrix can help individuals prioritize tasks and allocate their time more effectively. Time blocking is another technique that involves scheduling blocks of time for specific tasks and activities throughout the day, which can help individuals to stay focused and avoid distractions, while also making time for important tasks. By using these tools and techniques, individuals can effectively manage their time and prioritize tasks, leading to increased productivity and a greater sense of control over their lives.

CHAPTER 8

Building a Positive
and Productive Work Culture

Creating a positive and productive work culture is essential for the success of any organization. A positive work culture can improve employee morale, increase productivity, and decrease turnover rates. It can also create a sense of community and belonging among employees, resulting in a more collaborative and supportive workplace. Building a positive work culture requires a commitment from leadership and a willingness to prioritize employee well-being and job satisfaction. By fostering a culture of respect, transparency, and open communication, organizations can create a work environment where employees feel valued and motivated to contribute to the company's success.

At the heart of building a positive work culture is the recognition that employees are a company's most valuable asset. Organizations that prioritize their employees' well-being and development tend to have higher levels of job satisfaction, engagement, and retention. A positive work culture can be created through a range of practices, including promoting work-life balance, offering professional development opportunities, and providing meaningful recognition and rewards for employees' contributions. Additionally, a positive work culture is built on a foundation of open and honest communication, where employees feel heard and valued. By prioritizing these key principles, organizations can create a positive and productive work culture that benefits both employees and the company as a whole. In this chapter, we will explore the key principles and practices that can help organizations build and maintain a positive and productive work culture.

The Importance of Trust and Respect

Trust and respect are two of the most essential components of a positive and productive work culture. When employees feel that they can trust their colleagues and management, and that they are respected for their contributions and ideas, they are more likely to be engaged and committed to their work. Trust is built through open and honest communication, and by demonstrating that employees are valued and their concerns are heard and addressed. This can be achieved through regular check-ins, feedback sessions, and employee surveys, as well as by responding quickly and effectively to employee feedback and concerns. Respect, on the other hand, is built through recognizing and acknowledging employees' hard work and contributions, as well as by fostering a culture that values diversity and inclusion. This can include promoting diversity in hiring and promotion practices, offering cultural awareness training, and creating a workplace that is welcoming to all employees, regardless of their background.

A workplace that values trust and respect also encourages collaboration and teamwork. When employees feel that their ideas are valued and that they can work together with their colleagues to achieve common goals, they are more likely to be motivated and productive. Building trust and respect requires a long-term commitment from leadership, as it involves creating a culture that values and prioritizes these key principles. This can be achieved by modeling the behavior that is expected from employees, and by creating policies and practices that support a culture of trust and respect.

Leadership must also be willing to admit when mistakes have been made and take responsibility for their actions. This can help build trust among employees and demonstrate that leadership is committed to fostering a culture of transparency and accountability. Trust and respect are also built through consistency in behavior and decision-making. When employees feel that leadership is fair and consistent in their actions, they are more likely to trust in the organization and be committed to its goals.

One of the key benefits of a culture of trust and respect is increased employee engagement. When employees feel that their contributions are valued and their ideas are heard, they are more likely to be invested in their work and committed to the success of the organization. Another benefit of a culture of trust and respect is increased retention. When employees feel that they are part of a workplace that values them and their contributions, they are more likely to stay with the organization and contribute to its long-term success.

Building trust and respect also involves addressing issues of workplace harassment and discrimination. When employees feel that they are working in a safe and inclusive environment, they are more likely to trust their colleagues and management, and to be motivated and productive in their work. To build trust and respect, it is important to recognize and address any issues that may be hindering the creation of a positive work culture. This may involve investing in training and education for employees and management, and creating policies and practices that promote a culture of inclusion and respect.

Encouraging employees to take ownership of their work and empowering them to make decisions can also help build trust and respect. When employees feel that they have control over their work and that their contributions are valued, they are more likely to be invested in the success of the organization. It is also important to recognize that building trust and respect is an ongoing process that requires continuous evaluation and adjustment. Regular surveys and feedback sessions can help identify areas for improvement, and leadership should be willing to make changes to improve the work environment for employees.

Another key aspect of building trust and respect is ensuring that employees feel that their work is meaningful and contributes to the success of the organization. This can be achieved by providing clear goals and objectives, and by recognizing and rewarding employees for their hard work and contributions. Leaders can build trust and respect by involving employees in decision-making processes. When employees feel that their opinions and ideas are valued, they are more likely to be engaged and committed to their work.

Another important factor in building trust and respect is to foster a sense of community in the workplace. This can be achieved through team-building activities, social events, and volunteer opportunities. In order to build trust and respect, it is important to create a culture of open and honest communication. This means encouraging employees to share their thoughts and opinions, and listening actively to what they have to say. Another key element in building trust and respect is to establish clear expectations and goals. When employees have a clear understanding of what is expected of them, they are more likely to be motivated and committed to achieving those goals. It is also important to create an environment of mutual support and collaboration. When employees feel that they are part of a team that is working towards a common goal, they are more likely to feel invested in their work.

Trust and respect can also be built through recognition and appreciation. When employees feel that their hard work and contributions are acknowledged and valued, they are more likely to be motivated to continue performing at a high level. Leaders have a critical role to play in building trust and respect in the workplace. They must model the behavior they want to see in their employees, including being transparent, accountable, and respectful in their interactions with others.

Building trust and respect takes time and effort, but the benefits are significant. When employees feel that they can trust their colleagues and managers, they are more likely to be engaged, committed, and productive in their work. Conversely, a lack of trust and respect can lead to a toxic work environment. When employees do not feel valued or respected, they may become disengaged, unmotivated, and even resentful towards their colleagues and managers.

Trust and respect are also important for creating a sense of psychological safety in the workplace. When employees feel that they can speak up without fear of retribution, they are more likely to share their thoughts and ideas, which can lead to innovation and creativity. One way to build trust and respect is to establish clear boundaries and guidelines for behavior. This can include establishing a code of conduct, addressing inappropriate behavior, and promoting a culture of kindness and inclusivity.

Another way to build trust and respect is to offer opportunities for feedback and input. This can include regular check-ins, employee surveys, and focus groups to help identify areas for improvement and to gather input from employees on how to address these issues. Leaders can also build trust and respect by being transparent about the organization's goals and objectives, and by providing regular updates on progress towards these goals.

Building trust and respect also requires recognizing and addressing the underlying causes of conflict and tension in the workplace. This may include addressing issues of bias, discrimination, or inequity, and taking proactive steps to create a more inclusive and welcoming work environment. Another way to foster trust and respect is to establish clear lines of communication between management and employees. This can involve regularly scheduled meetings or check-ins, as well as providing employees with the opportunity to give feedback or ask questions.

Creating a culture of trust and respect also involves setting clear expectations for behavior and conduct. This can be achieved through the creation of a code of conduct or other policies that outline expected behaviors and consequences for violations. Trust and respect can also be built through transparency in decision-making. When employees feel that they understand why decisions are being made, they are more likely to trust that those decisions are in the best interest of the organization.

Finally, it is important to remember that building a culture of trust and respect takes time and effort. It requires a commitment from leadership and a willingness to listen and respond to employee feedback. However, the benefits of a positive and productive work culture, including increased employee engagement, retention, and productivity, make it well worth the investment.

Effective Communication Strategies

Effective communication is critical to building a positive and productive work culture. Employees who feel that they can communicate openly and honestly with their managers are more likely to be engaged and productive. In this chapter, we will discuss how to establish open lines of communication between employees and management, and how to ensure that communication is clear, respectful, and productive.

Establishing Regular Check-Ins: Regular check-ins are a great way to establish open lines of communication between employees and management. These meetings can be informal, such as a quick chat over coffee, or more formal, such as a scheduled one-on-one meeting. By establishing regular check-ins, managers can get to know their employees better and gain insight into their goals, concerns, and ideas.

Creating an Open-Door Policy: An open-door policy is another way to establish open lines of communication between employees and management. This policy encourages employees to approach their managers with questions or concerns, and assures them that their concerns will be heard and addressed.

Encouraging Employee Feedback: Encouraging employee feedback is another important way to establish open lines of communication. This can involve soliciting feedback through surveys or suggestion boxes, or simply encouraging employees to speak up and share their thoughts and ideas.

Providing Communication Training: Effective communication is a skill that can be learned, and providing communication training to employees and managers can help to establish clear, respectful, and productive communication. This training can cover topics such as active listening, conflict resolution, and giving and receiving feedback.

Using Technology to Facilitate Communication: In today's digital age, there are many tools and technologies that can be used to facilitate communication between employees and management. This can include chat apps, video conferencing, or project management software. By using technology to facilitate communication, managers can keep employees informed and connected, regardless of their physical location.

Creating Communication Guidelines: Clear communication guidelines can help to ensure that communication is clear, respectful, and productive. These guidelines can outline expectations for communication, such as using respectful language and active listening, and can provide tips and strategies for effective communication.

Encouraging Diversity of Thought: Finally, it is important to encourage diversity of thought in the workplace. This means valuing the unique perspectives and ideas of all employees, regardless of their background or position. By encouraging diversity of thought, managers can create a workplace that is innovative, inclusive, and productive.

Establishing open lines of communication between employees and management is critical to building a positive and productive work culture. By creating an environment that encourages open communication, provides opportunities for feedback, and values diversity of thought, managers can create a workplace where employees are engaged, productive, and invested in the success of the organization. By prioritizing effective communication, managers can build a workplace that is respectful, productive, and inclusive.

Strategies for Promoting Work-Life Balance

In today's fast-paced work environment, achieving work-life balance can be a challenge. However, it is essential to create a work environment that values work-life balance, as this can have a significant impact on employee well-being, productivity, and job satisfaction. In this section, we will discuss the importance of work-life balance, and how to create a workplace culture that supports it.

The Benefits of Work-Life Balance: A healthy work-life balance is associated with a range of benefits, including improved mental and physical health, increased job satisfaction and engagement, and higher productivity. By prioritizing work-life balance, employers can create a workplace that is more inclusive, supportive, and productive.

Common Barriers to Work-Life Balance: Despite the many benefits of work-life balance, there are often barriers that prevent employees from achieving it. These can include long working hours, excessive workload, inflexible work arrangements, and a lack of support from management. By identifying and addressing these barriers, employers can create a more supportive work environment that values employee well-being.

Once you understand the importance of work-life balance, the next step is to create a work environment that supports it. Next, we will discuss some strategies for creating a work environment that values work-life balance and supports employee well-being.

Flexible Work Arrangements: Offering flexible work arrangements, such as flexible working hours, part-time work, or telecommuting, can be an effective way to support work-life balance. These arrangements allow employees to better manage their work and personal responsibilities, and can improve job satisfaction, productivity, and retention. Time Off: Providing ample time off, such as vacation time, sick leave, and parental leave, is another way to support work-life balance. This time off can be used to recharge, spend time with family, or take care of personal responsibilities, all of which can contribute to employee well-being and job satisfaction.

Employee Wellness Programs: Employee wellness programs, such as fitness classes, mindfulness training, and mental health support, can be an effective way to support employee well-being and work-life balance. By providing these resources, employers can help employees manage stress and maintain a healthy work-life balance.

Clear Communication: Clear communication is essential for creating a work environment that supports work-life balance. Employers should communicate their expectations for work-life balance, provide resources and support for achieving it, and ensure that employees are aware of their rights to time off and other benefits.

Lead by Example: Finally, employers should lead by example when it comes to work-life balance. This means modeling healthy work habits, such as taking breaks and using vacation time, and demonstrating a commitment to employee well-being. By leading by example, employers can create a workplace culture that values work-life balance and supports employee well-being.

Creating a work environment that values work-life balance is essential for supporting employee well-being, productivity, and job satisfaction. By understanding the importance of work-life balance, identifying common barriers to achieving it, and implementing strategies that support it, employers can create a more inclusive, supportive, and productive work environment. By prioritizing work-life balance, employers can create a workplace culture that values employee well-being and supports their personal and professional goals.

The Role of Recognition and Rewards

Recognizing and rewarding employees for their hard work and contributions is critical for promoting a positive and productive work culture. This is because when employees feel valued and appreciated, they are more likely to be engaged, motivated, and committed to their work. In this section, we will discuss the importance of recognizing and rewarding employees, and why this is critical for promoting a positive and productive work culture.

Boosts Morale: Recognizing and rewarding employees can boost morale and increase job satisfaction. This is because when employees feel appreciated and valued, they are more likely to feel motivated and engaged in their work.

Increases Productivity: Recognizing and rewarding employees for their hard work and contributions can also increase productivity. This is because when employees are motivated, they are more likely to put in extra effort and go above and beyond in their work.

Improves Retention: Recognizing and rewarding employees can also improve retention rates. When employees feel valued and appreciated, they are more likely to stay with the company and continue to be productive and engaged in their work.

Now that we understand the importance of recognizing and rewarding employees, the next step is to identify strategies for doing so. In this section, we will discuss some effective strategies for recognizing and rewarding employees, and why these strategies are critical for promoting a positive and productive work culture.

Provide Feedback: Providing feedback is one of the most effective ways to recognize and reward employees. By providing regular feedback, employees can gain a better understanding of their strengths and areas for improvement, which can help them to improve their performance and feel more valued in their work.

Offer Employee Perks: Employee perks, such as free lunches, gym memberships, or company events, can be an effective way to recognize and reward employees. These perks can help to create a more positive and supportive work environment and improve employee morale.

Recognize Achievements: Recognizing and celebrating employee achievements is another effective way to recognize and reward employees. This can be done through public recognition, such as an announcement in a team meeting, or through more formal rewards, such as bonuses or promotions.

Encourage Employee Development: Encouraging employee development is another way to recognize and reward employees. This can be done through training programs, mentoring, or other professional development opportunities, which can help employees to improve their skills and advance in their careers.

Recognizing and rewarding employees for their hard work and contributions is critical for promoting a positive and productive work culture. By boosting morale, increasing productivity, and improving retention rates, recognizing, and rewarding employees can have a significant impact on the success of a company. By providing feedback, offering employee perks, recognizing achievements, and encouraging employee development, employers can create a work environment that values and supports its employees, which can contribute to a more positive and productive workplace culture.

Creating a Culture of Learning and Growth

As an employer, one of the most important things you can do to retain and motivate your employees is to provide them with opportunities for professional development and growth. This can take many forms, such as training programs, mentorship, coaching, and on-the-job learning experiences. Here are some strategies for providing your employees with opportunities for professional development and growth:

Develop a culture of continuous learning: Encourage your employees to embrace the idea of continuous learning and growth. This can be achieved by providing them with regular feedback, setting clear goals and expectations, and offering support and resources for their development.

Create individual development plans: Work with your employees to create individual development plans that align with their career goals and interests. These plans should include specific training, learning, and development opportunities that will help them grow professionally.

Offer training and development programs: Provide your employees with access to training and development programs that are relevant to their roles and responsibilities. This can include both internal and external training programs, workshops, and conferences.

Provide mentorship and coaching: Pair your employees with experienced mentors or coaches who can provide guidance and support as they develop their skills and knowledge.

Encourage on-the-job learning: Provide your employees with opportunities to learn on the job through stretch assignments, job rotations, and cross-functional projects.

Providing your employees with opportunities for professional development and growth is not just important for their individual growth and success; it can also have a significant impact on the engagement and motivation of your workforce as a whole. Here are some ways that professional development can foster a sense of engagement and motivation in the workplace:

Increased job satisfaction: When employees feel that their employer is invested in their professional development and growth, they are more likely to be satisfied with their jobs and feel that they are making a meaningful contribution to the organization.

Enhanced skills and knowledge: By providing your employees with opportunities to develop new skills and knowledge, you are helping them to become more competent and confident in their roles. This can lead to increased productivity, better quality of work, and a stronger sense of job security.

Career advancement opportunities: When employees feel that their employer is invested in their growth and development, they are more likely to stay with the organization and seek out career advancement opportunities. This can help you to retain top talent and build a strong and motivated workforce.

Improved morale: Providing opportunities for professional development and growth can also improve morale and create a more positive work environment. When employees feel that they are valued and supported, they are more likely to be engaged and motivated at work.

Providing your employees with opportunities for professional development and growth is a win-win situation for both the employer and employee. By investing in your employees' development, you can foster a sense of engagement and motivation in the workplace, retain top talent, and build a strong and productive workforce.

While providing professional development opportunities can greatly benefit both employees and employers, it's important to have a solid plan in place for implementing these opportunities. Here are some best practices to keep in mind when implementing professional development opportunities in your workplace:

Identify the needs of your employees: Before implementing any professional development programs, it's important to identify the specific needs of your employees. This can be achieved through surveys, focus groups, or one-on-one meetings with employees. Understanding their needs and goals will help you create a more effective and targeted professional development plan.

Communicate the benefits of professional development: Make sure your employees understand the benefits of professional development and how it can help them grow in their careers. Be transparent about how these opportunities align with their career goals and the company's objectives.

Encourage participation: To ensure maximum participation in professional development opportunities, it's important to make them accessible and flexible. Offer a range of training programs and scheduling options to accommodate the diverse needs of your workforce.

Provide ongoing support and resources: Professional development opportunities shouldn't be a one-time event. It's important to provide ongoing support and resources to employees as they continue to develop their skills and knowledge. This can include access to online resources, mentorship, coaching, and performance feedback.

Evaluate the effectiveness of your programs: To ensure your professional development programs are effective, it's important to evaluate their impact on employee engagement and performance. Collect feedback from employees and track performance metrics to assess the ROI of your professional development initiatives.

By following these best practices, you can create a culture of continuous learning and growth in your workplace, and provide your employees with the support they need to achieve their professional goals.

Application

A positive and productive work culture is essential for any organization that wants to attract and retain top talent, and achieve its goals. A strong work culture can help to create a sense of community, foster collaboration and innovation, and increase employee engagement and motivation. Building a positive and productive work culture doesn't happen overnight, and requires a concerted effort from leadership and employees alike. However, with the right tools and strategies, it's possible to create a work culture that is supportive, inclusive, and inspiring. In this guide, we'll explore some of the key applications and strategies for building a positive and productive work culture, and discuss how you can implement them in your own organization. In order to apply the knowledge and insights gained from chapter eight, managers can employ the following:

Employee recognition programs: One way to foster a positive and productive work culture is by implementing employee recognition programs. These can be as simple as a shout-out during a team meeting, or as formal as an awards program that recognizes top performers.

Recognizing employees for their hard work and contributions helps to build a sense of community and fosters a culture of positivity.

Communication channels: Another way to build a positive work culture is to establish clear communication channels. This can involve regular meetings, email updates, or an intranet system that allows for easy communication and collaboration. By keeping employees in the loop and providing them with the information they need to do their jobs, you can help them feel more engaged and invested in the success of the organization.

Flexibility and work-life balance: Employees who feel that they have a good work-life balance are more likely to be productive and engaged. By offering flexible work arrangements, such as the option to work from home or to adjust their schedules, you can help employees feel more in control of their work and personal lives. This can result in a more positive and productive work culture.

Training and development programs: Providing employees with opportunities for growth and development can help to build a positive work culture. By investing in your employees' professional development, you show them that you value their contributions and want to help them achieve their career goals. This can help to increase employee engagement and productivity.

Wellness initiatives: A focus on employee wellness can also help to build a positive work culture. This can involve offering wellness programs, such as gym memberships or yoga classes, as well as initiatives that promote healthy eating and stress management. By prioritizing employee wellness, you can create a workplace that supports and values its employees.

Diversity and inclusion initiatives: Building a positive and productive work culture also involves creating a workplace that is inclusive and values diversity. This can involve implementing policies that support diversity and inclusion, such as hiring practices that promote diversity and sensitivity training for employees. By fostering a culture of respect and inclusivity, you can help all employees feel valued and supported. Employee feedback programs: Finally, building a positive and productive work culture involves soliciting and acting on employee feedback. By providing employees with the opportunity to give feedback on their work environment and implementing changes based on that feedback, you can help create a workplace that is more engaging, productive, and positive.

Summary

Building a positive and productive work culture is essential for the success of any organization. It involves creating an environment that supports employee well-being, encourages collaboration and open communication, and recognizes and rewards employee contributions. By promoting a positive and productive work culture, organizations can improve employee morale, increase productivity, and foster a sense of community and teamwork among employees.

To build a positive and productive work culture, organizations should prioritize strategies such as establishing open lines of communication between employees and management, creating a work environment that values work-life balance, recognizing and rewarding employee contributions, promoting diversity and inclusion, and fostering a sense of community and teamwork. By implementing these strategies, organizations can create a work culture that is supportive, inclusive, and empowering, which can lead to increased employee engagement, job satisfaction, and overall organizational success.

CHAPTER 9

Adapting to Change
and Embracing Innovation

In today's fast-paced and ever-changing world, the ability to adapt to change and embrace innovation has become a critical skill for individuals and organizations. As new technologies and ways of doing business emerge, those who can quickly adapt and innovate are more likely to thrive and succeed. However, adapting to change and embracing innovation can be challenging, and many individuals and organizations struggle to keep up with the pace of change.

As the world continues to evolve at a rapid pace, those who fail to adapt risk being left behind. Adapting to change and embracing innovation requires individuals and organizations to be flexible, resilient, and willing to take risks. It also requires a willingness to learn and to continuously improve. In this chapter, we will explore the importance of adapting to change and embracing innovation, and provide practical strategies for doing so.

One of the key strategies for adapting to change and embracing innovation is to cultivate a growth mindset. This involves seeing challenges and setbacks as opportunities to learn and grow, rather than as failures. By adopting a growth mindset, individuals and organizations can become more resilient, creative, and adaptable, and better equipped to navigate the challenges of a rapidly changing world. Another important strategy for adapting to change and embracing innovation is to embrace experimentation. This involves trying new things, taking risks, and being open to new ideas and approaches. By experimenting with new ideas and approaches, individuals and organizations can learn what works and what doesn't, and make adjustments as needed. This can lead to new insights, discoveries, and innovations, and help individuals and organizations stay ahead of the curve.

Finally, collaboration is a powerful tool for adapting to change and embracing innovation. By working together and sharing knowledge and resources, individuals and organizations can leverage the strengths and expertise of others, and create innovative solutions to complex problems. Collaboration can also help to build a sense of community and shared purpose, which can be a powerful motivator for change and innovation.

In this chapter, we will explore strategies for adapting to change and embracing innovation, including the importance of a growth mindset, the role of experimentation, and the power of collaboration. We will also discuss how individuals and organizations can stay ahead of the curve and remain competitive in a rapidly changing world.

Cultivating a Growth Mindset

Seeing challenges as opportunities for growth

Understanding the growth mindset: In this section, we will explore the concept of the growth mindset, including its origins and the research behind it. We will explain how the growth mindset differs from a fixed mindset, and why cultivating a growth mindset is critical for adapting to change and embracing innovation. We will also provide examples of individuals and organizations that have successfully cultivated a growth mindset, and the benefits they have seen as a result.

The concept of the growth mindset was first introduced by psychologist Carol Dweck in her book "Mindset: The New Psychology of Success." The growth mindset is the belief that one's abilities and intelligence can be developed through dedication and hard work. This is in contrast to a fixed mindset, which is the belief that abilities and intelligence are innate and cannot be changed. Dweck's research has shown that individuals with a growth mindset are more likely to take on challenges, persist in the face of obstacles, and ultimately achieve greater success than those with a fixed mindset.

The benefits of cultivating a growth mindset are numerous. For individuals, it means being open to new ideas and experiences, and embracing challenges as opportunities for growth. It also means being more resilient in the face of setbacks, and more likely to succeed in the long run. For organizations, a growth mindset can lead to greater innovation, increased productivity, and a more engaged and motivated workforce.

One example of an individual who has successfully cultivated a growth mindset is Microsoft CEO Satya Nadella. In his book "Hit Refresh," Nadella describes his own journey of personal and professional growth, including his experiences navigating the rapidly changing landscape of the tech industry. Nadella emphasizes the importance of continuous learning and a willingness to embrace new challenges, both for himself and for his organization. Under Nadella's leadership, Microsoft has seen a significant shift in culture and innovation, with a focus on collaboration and a growth mindset. Another example of an organization that has successfully cultivated a growth mindset is the online shoe retailer Zappos. In her book "Delivering Happiness," Zappos CEO Tony Hsieh describes the company's culture of continuous learning and experimentation. Hsieh emphasizes the importance of creating a culture where employees are encouraged to take risks and learn from failure, and where innovation is celebrated as a key driver of success. As a result, Zappos has become known for its exceptional customer service and innovative approach to business.

Research has shown that cultivating a growth mindset can have a number of benefits for individuals and organizations. For example, a study published in the Journal of Personality and Social Psychology found that individuals with a growth mindset are more likely to seek out feedback and develop stronger relationships with their peers. Another study, published in the Journal of Business and Psychology, found that organizations with a growth mindset are more likely to innovate and adapt to changing market conditions.

Overall, the concept of the growth mindset has become increasingly important in a world where change and innovation are constant. By embracing the belief that abilities and intelligence can be developed through hard work and dedication, individuals and organizations can become more resilient, adaptable, and ultimately more successful.

Overcoming resistance to change: Strategies for managing uncertainty and risk. In this section, we will explore the common reasons people resist change, and provide strategies for managing uncertainty and risk. We will discuss the importance of communicating clearly and openly with employees during times of change, and how to manage their fears and concerns. We will also cover the role of leadership in managing change, including the importance of modeling the desired behavior, setting clear expectations, and providing support and resources to employees during times of transition.

Change is an inevitable part of life and the workplace. However, many people resist change for a variety of reasons, such as fear of the unknown, loss of control, and the potential for failure. To manage change effectively, it is important to understand the common reasons people resist change and develop strategies to address them. By doing so, you can help employees navigate uncertainty and risk, and ultimately build a culture that is more open to change and innovation.

One common reason people resist change is fear of the unknown. This can include uncertainty about how the change will affect their job, their responsibilities, and their future. To address this fear, it is important to communicate clearly and openly with employees about the reasons for the change, what the change will entail, and how it will benefit the organization and its employees in the long term. By providing as much information as possible, you can help employees feel more informed and prepared for the change.

Another common reason people resist change is loss of control. People like to feel in control of their work and their environment, and change can disrupt this sense of control. To address this fear, it is important to involve employees in the change process as much as possible. This can include seeking their input and feedback, providing opportunities for them to participate in the change, and allowing them to take ownership of the process. By involving employees in the change process, you can help them feel more invested in the change and less threatened by it.

The potential for failure is another common reason people resist change. Change can be risky, and there is always the possibility that it will not work out as planned. To address this fear, it is important to manage uncertainty and risk by developing a clear plan for the change, identifying potential risks and challenges, and developing strategies to mitigate them. By providing a clear plan and addressing potential risks, you can help employees feel more confident and prepared for the change.

In managing change, it is also important to communicate openly and honestly with employees about their fears and concerns. This can include acknowledging their concerns, addressing them directly, and providing support and resources to help them navigate the change. By communicating openly and honestly, you can build trust and foster a culture of transparency that is more open to change and innovation.

Finally, leadership plays a critical role in managing change. Leaders should model the desired behavior, set clear expectations for employees, and provide the necessary support and resources to help them navigate the change. By demonstrating a commitment to change and providing the necessary resources and support, leaders can help employees feel more invested in the change and more prepared to adapt to the new environment. Overall, managing change requires a combination of effective communication, risk management, and leadership support, and a focus on addressing the common reasons people resist change.

Building a culture of innovation: Creating an environment that supports creativity and experimentation. In this section, we will discuss the importance of building a culture of innovation, including how to create an environment that supports creativity and experimentation. We will explore the key characteristics of innovative organizations, and provide examples of companies that have successfully fostered a culture of innovation. We will also provide practical strategies for creating an environment that supports innovation, including encouraging idea generation, providing resources and tools to support experimentation, and creating a feedback loop for continuous improvement.

Creating an environment that supports creativity and experimentation is crucial for organizations looking to stay ahead of the curve and remain competitive in today's rapidly evolving business landscape. To do this, it's important to build a culture of innovation - one that encourages experimentation, rewards creativity, and values risk-taking.

One key characteristic of innovative organizations is their willingness to take risks and experiment. They understand that not every idea will be a winner, but they're willing to invest time and resources in trying new things in the pursuit of new solutions and breakthroughs.

Another important characteristic of innovative organizations is a willingness to challenge the status quo. This means questioning long-held assumptions and approaches, and being willing to pivot or change direction when necessary. It also means being open to feedback and using it to continuously improve.

Many companies have successfully fostered a culture of innovation. For example, Google encourages employees to spend 20% of their time working on projects outside of their regular job duties, which has led to the development of innovative products such as Gmail and Google Maps. Similarly, Amazon has a culture of experimentation and encourages employees to take risks and test new ideas, which has led to the company's success in areas like cloud computing and e-commerce.

To create an environment that supports innovation, it's important to encourage idea generation and provide resources and tools to support experimentation. This can be done through brainstorming sessions, hackathons, or other creative exercises that give employees the space to think outside the box and generate new ideas. It's also important to provide the resources and support needed to test these ideas, whether that's through funding, access to technology or other resources, or the ability to work with cross-functional teams.

Finally, creating a feedback loop is crucial for continuous improvement. This means collecting feedback on ideas and experiments, analyzing the results, and using that information to refine and improve future efforts. It's also important to communicate openly and honestly with employees about the results of experiments and the company's overall innovation strategy, to help build trust and buy-in among the team.

In short, creating a culture of innovation requires a willingness to take risks and experiment, a commitment to challenging the status quo, and a focus on idea generation, experimentation, and continuous improvement. By creating an environment that supports these key elements, organizations can drive innovation and stay ahead of the competition.

Building a culture of innovation: Creating an environment that supports creativity and experimentation In this section, we will discuss the importance of building a culture of innovation, including how to create an environment that supports creativity and experimentation. We will explore the key characteristics of innovative organizations, and provide examples of companies that have successfully fostered a culture of innovation. We will also provide practical strategies for creating an environment that supports innovation, including encouraging idea generation, providing resources and tools to support experimentation, and creating a feedback loop for continuous improvement.

Creating an environment that supports creativity and experimentation is crucial for businesses looking to stay competitive in today's rapidly changing marketplace. To do this, organizations must build a culture of innovation that fosters creativity, experimentation, and continuous learning.

One of the key characteristics of innovative organizations is a willingness to take risks and embrace failure. Companies that are able to do this create an environment where employees feel free to try new things without fear of retribution, which encourages experimentation and creativity. For example, Google has famously adopted a "fail fast, fail often" mentality, encouraging employees to experiment and iterate on their ideas until they find success.

Another important characteristic of innovative organizations is a focus on collaboration and teamwork. By working together, employees are able to bounce ideas off one another and build on each other's strengths, which leads to more creative solutions. Companies like IDEO and Pixar are known for their collaborative work environments, where cross-functional teams are brought together to tackle complex challenges. To create an environment that supports innovation, organizations must encourage idea generation and provide the resources and tools necessary to support experimentation. This might include setting up brainstorming sessions, creating innovation labs or maker spaces, or providing employees with access to cutting-edge technology and other resources.

Creating a feedback loop for continuous improvement is also crucial for fostering a culture of innovation. By regularly soliciting feedback from employees and customers, organizations can identify areas for improvement and adjust their approach accordingly. Companies like Amazon and Netflix are known for their data-driven approach to innovation, using customer feedback to inform their product development and decision-making.

Ultimately, building a culture of innovation is a continuous process that requires ongoing commitment from leaders and employees at all levels of the organization. By embracing risk-taking, collaboration, and continuous learning, businesses can create an environment that supports creativity and experimentation, driving long-term success and growth.

The power of collaboration: Leveraging diverse perspectives and expertise to drive innovation. In this section, we will explore the power of collaboration in driving innovation. We will discuss the benefits of working in diverse teams, including the ability to bring a variety of perspectives and expertise to a problem, and the ability to challenge assumptions and think outside the box. We will also discuss the importance of creating a collaborative work environment, including how to build trust and respect among team members, and how to leverage technology to support collaboration. By the end of this section, readers will have a clear understanding of the importance of collaboration in driving innovation, and practical strategies for creating a collaborative work environment.

Leveraging diverse perspectives and expertise to drive innovation is an essential aspect of building a culture of innovation. Collaborating with others who bring different perspectives, knowledge, and skills to the table can lead to more creative and effective solutions to complex problems. Working in diverse teams enables organizations to leverage the power of collective intelligence and promote a more inclusive workplace. When individuals with diverse backgrounds and experiences come together, they are better equipped to generate innovative solutions that address a wide range of challenges.

Building a collaborative work environment is a crucial factor in leveraging diverse perspectives and expertise to drive innovation. Collaboration can be achieved through creating a culture that values open communication and encourages individuals to share their ideas, opinions, and experiences. This can be achieved through team-building activities, open-door policies, and cross-functional projects. By creating a collaborative work environment, organizations can break down silos, build bridges between departments, and foster a culture of open communication.

Another critical aspect of leveraging diverse perspectives and expertise is building trust and respect among team members. When people feel respected and valued, they are more likely to share their ideas and engage in productive collaboration. Building trust and respect can be achieved through creating an inclusive and welcoming work environment that celebrates diversity and promotes open dialogue. Additionally, organizations can implement training programs and workshops that promote cultural awareness and encourage understanding of different perspectives. Leveraging technology is also essential in promoting collaboration and driving innovation. Modern technology tools, such as video conferencing, cloud-based collaboration software, and project management tools, can help to break down barriers between team members, facilitate real-time collaboration, and support remote work. By providing employees with the right technology tools, organizations can enable teams to work together more effectively, regardless of their location.

Finally, successful collaboration requires effective communication. This includes active listening, clear articulation of ideas, and being open to feedback. Leaders can model effective communication by providing clear instructions, setting expectations, and providing constructive feedback. Organizations can also encourage a culture of continuous learning and improvement by providing training and development opportunities that focus on improving communication skills. By leveraging diverse perspectives and expertise to drive innovation, organizations can foster a culture of innovation that drives growth and success.

The Role of Experimentation in Adapting to Change and Embracing Innovation

Experimentation is a critical component of adapting to change and embracing innovation. It allows organizations to test new ideas, products, and processes in a low-risk environment, and make adjustments based on real-world feedback. Experimentation can help companies to quickly identify what works and what doesn't, and make informed decisions about how to move forward.

To be effective, experimentation requires a willingness to take risks, and an openness to failure. Organizations that are afraid to fail may be reluctant to experiment, which can stifle innovation and limit growth. To create a culture of experimentation, leaders need to encourage their employees to take risks and be willing to try new things. They also need to be willing to embrace failure as an opportunity to learn and grow, and to use the insights gained from failed experiments to inform future decisions.

Another key component of successful experimentation is the ability to collect and analyze data. In order to make informed decisions about how to move forward, organizations need to be able to track and measure the results of their experiments. This requires the ability to collect data in a structured and systematic way, and to use this data to make informed decisions about which ideas to pursue and which to abandon.

Experimentation can take many forms, from small-scale tests of new products or services, to larger experiments that involve fundamental changes to the way a business operates. One common approach to experimentation is the use of agile methodologies, which involve breaking down complex projects into smaller, more manageable tasks, and testing each component as it is developed. This approach allows organizations to make changes quickly, and to pivot as needed based on the results of their experiments.

Finally, successful experimentation requires a commitment to continuous improvement. Organizations that are able to adapt quickly to changing circumstances and to embrace new ideas and approaches are more likely to succeed in today's fast-paced business environment. By fostering a culture of experimentation and continuous improvement, companies can stay ahead of the curve and remain competitive in an ever-changing marketplace.

Here are some references that explore the role of experimentation in adapting to change and embracing innovation. These sources provide insights into the benefits of experimentation, including the ability to learn from failure, and how to create an environment that supports experimentation. They also offer practical strategies for conducting experiments, including how to measure and evaluate results, and how to leverage experimentation to drive continuous improvement. Whether you are looking to drive innovation within your organization, or simply seeking to develop your skills in experimentation and adaptability, these references can provide valuable guidance and inspiration:

1. Dweck, C. S. (2017). Mindset: Changing the way you think to fulfil your potential. Hachette UK.

2. HBR's 10 Must Reads on Change Management. (2011). Harvard Business Press. Osterwalder, A., & Pigneur, Y. (2010). Business model generation: a handbook for visionaries, game changers, and challengers. John Wiley & Sons.

3. Pink, D. H. (2009). Drive: The surprising truth about what motivates us. Penguin.

4. Sutton, R. I., & Rao, H. (2014). Scaling up excellence: Getting to more without settling for less. Crown Business.

5. The Lean Startup: How Today's Entrepreneurs Use Continuous Innovation to Create Radically Successful Businesses by Eric Ries.

6. The Innovator's Dilemma: When New Technologies Cause Great Firms to Fail by Clayton M. Christensen.

7. Creativity, Inc.: Overcoming the Unseen Forces That Stand in the Way of True Inspiration by Ed Catmull.

8. The Design of Business: Why Design Thinking is the Next Competitive Advantage by Roger Martin.

Design Thinking: Integrating Innovation, Customer Experience, and Brand Value by Thomas Lockwood.

Overcoming Resistance to Change

Strategies for managing uncertainty and risk

Overcoming resistance to change is often one of the biggest challenges that leaders and organizations face. People are naturally resistant to change, and it can be difficult to get them to embrace new ways of doing things. However, by understanding the reasons behind this resistance and implementing strategies to manage uncertainty and risk, organizations can help their employees navigate change more effectively.

One common reason people resist change is fear of the unknown. When faced with an unfamiliar situation, people often become anxious and worry about what might happen. To overcome this fear, leaders can provide clear communication about the changes that are happening, including the reasons behind them and the benefits they will bring. By providing a clear roadmap and helping people understand what to expect, leaders can help ease fears and build confidence in the process.

Another reason people resist change is a lack of control. People often feel more comfortable when they are in control of their environment and their work, and change can disrupt this sense of control. To help manage this, leaders can involve employees in the change process by soliciting feedback and input, giving them a sense of ownership in the process. By involving employees in the decision-making process, leaders can help them feel more in control and invested in the change.

People also resist change because they don't see the benefits of it. They may feel that the current way of doing things is working just fine, and don't see the need for change. To address this, leaders can provide clear, tangible benefits of the change, such as increased productivity, reduced costs, or improved work-life balance. By showing people how the change will benefit them, leaders can help employees understand the value of the change and become more supportive of it.

Another strategy for managing resistance to change is to break it down into smaller, more manageable pieces. Rather than implementing a large-scale change all at once, leaders can break it down into smaller, incremental changes. This allows employees to adapt to each change more easily and gives them time to adjust before the next change comes.

It's also important for leaders to provide support and resources to employees during times of change. This can include additional training, coaching, or mentoring to help employees develop the skills they need to be successful in the new environment. Leaders can also provide emotional support and counseling to help employees manage their fears and concerns during the transition.

Leaders can also help employees overcome resistance to change by building a culture of trust and transparency. When employees trust their leaders and feel that they are being honest and transparent, they are more likely to be supportive of changes. Leaders can build this culture by being open and honest about the reasons for the change, communicating frequently and clearly, and involving employees in decision-making processes. Another strategy for managing resistance to change is to create a sense of urgency. When people feel that change is necessary and urgent, they are more likely to be supportive of it. Leaders can create a sense of urgency by communicating the need for change clearly and effectively, and by emphasizing the risks of not changing.

Finally, leaders can manage resistance to change by setting clear expectations and holding employees accountable for meeting them. By setting clear goals and metrics, leaders can help employees understand what is expected of them and track their progress. When employees see that their work is making a difference, they are more likely to be supportive of change and to work hard to make it happen.

Overcoming resistance to change is a critical skill for leaders and organizations. By understanding the reasons behind resistance and implementing effective strategies for managing uncertainty and risk, leaders can help their employees navigate change more effectively and ensure that the organization can adapt and innovate in the face of new challenges.

Building a Culture of Innovation

Creating an environment that supports creativity and experimentation

Building a culture of innovation is critical to staying competitive and relevant in today's fast-paced and constantly evolving business world. One of the keys to building such a culture is creating an environment that supports creativity and experimentation. In this section, we will explore the importance of building a culture of innovation and provide practical strategies for creating an environment that supports creativity and experimentation.

One of the key characteristics of innovative organizations is that they encourage idea generation. These companies create an environment where employees feel comfortable sharing their ideas, regardless of how unconventional or risky they may seem. They recognize that innovation often comes from unexpected sources and that the best ideas may come from people outside of the traditional management hierarchy. Therefore, it's essential to create an open and inclusive environment where everyone feels empowered to contribute their ideas.

Another critical component of a culture of innovation is providing resources and tools to support experimentation. Innovative organizations recognize that experimentation is essential to innovation and growth. Therefore, they provide their employees with the necessary resources and tools to experiment and take risks. They understand that not all experiments will succeed, but that the lessons learned from those failures can be just as valuable as the successes.

Creating a feedback loop for continuous improvement is another essential aspect of building a culture of innovation. This means collecting data and feedback from customers and employees, and using that information to refine and improve products, services, and processes. Innovative organizations are constantly looking for ways to improve and enhance their offerings, and they use data and feedback to drive those improvements.

To create an environment that supports creativity and experimentation, it's also crucial to encourage collaboration and teamwork. Innovative organizations understand that the best ideas often come from a team effort, and they work to build trust and respect among team members. They recognize the importance of diversity and inclusion, and they encourage diverse perspectives and ideas.

Innovative organizations also leverage technology to support collaboration and experimentation. They use tools and software to facilitate communication, brainstorming, and ideation. They invest in technologies that support experimentation, such as virtual and augmented reality, machine learning, and artificial intelligence. They recognize that technology is an essential tool for driving innovation and growth.

Another critical element of building a culture of innovation is providing leadership that fosters creativity and experimentation. Innovative leaders model the desired behavior by encouraging risk-taking, celebrating failure, and rewarding experimentation. They set clear expectations for innovation and growth and provide the necessary support and resources to achieve those goals. Innovative organizations also create an environment that supports learning and development. They recognize that innovation often requires new skills and knowledge, and they provide their employees with opportunities for training and development. They encourage their employees to learn new things and explore new ideas, and they invest in their professional growth and development.

Building a culture of innovation requires creating an environment that supports creativity and experimentation. This means encouraging idea generation, providing resources and tools for experimentation, creating a feedback loop for continuous improvement, encouraging collaboration and teamwork, leveraging technology, providing leadership that fosters innovation, and supporting learning and development. By implementing these strategies, organizations can create an environment that supports innovation and growth, stay competitive and relevant in today's rapidly evolving business world.

The Power of Collaboration

Leveraging diverse perspectives and expertise to drive innovation

The power of collaboration cannot be understated when it comes to driving innovation. Collaboration between individuals and teams with diverse perspectives and expertise is critical for generating new ideas and solutions to complex problems. In today's fast-paced business environment, the ability to innovate is essential to remain competitive and relevant. Therefore, managers must be effective at leveraging diverse perspectives and expertise to drive innovation.

One of the key benefits of working in diverse teams is the ability to bring a variety of perspectives and expertise to a problem. When individuals with different backgrounds, experiences, and skills work together, they can identify opportunities and challenges that might have been missed if only one perspective was considered. For example, a team consisting of individuals with technical, creative, and business backgrounds can leverage their unique skills to create a more comprehensive and innovative solution.

However, working in diverse teams can also present challenges. Differences in communication styles, cultural backgrounds, and personalities can create barriers to effective collaboration. Therefore, it is essential for managers to create a collaborative work environment that promotes trust and respect among team members. This can be achieved by fostering an open and inclusive culture where all team members feel valued and heard.

Managers can also leverage technology to support collaboration. With the right tools, teams can communicate and share ideas easily, regardless of their location or time zone. Video conferencing, instant messaging, and project management software are all examples of technology that can support collaboration and innovation.

To leverage diverse perspectives and expertise effectively, managers must also be open to new ideas and willing to challenge assumptions. This means encouraging team members to share their thoughts and ideas, even if they go against the status quo. It also means creating a safe environment where team members can fail and learn from their mistakes without fear of repercussions.

Another key role for managers in leveraging diverse perspectives and expertise is to facilitate effective communication. This means ensuring that team members are communicating clearly and effectively, and that all ideas are being heard and considered. It also means mediating conflicts and disagreements that may arise, and finding ways to resolve them in a constructive and respectful manner.

In addition to facilitating effective communication, managers must also provide resources and support to enable innovation. This may include providing training and development opportunities to team members, as well as access to the latest technologies and tools. It may also mean providing a safe space for experimentation and risk-taking, where team members can try new things without fear of failure. As a manager, it's your role to foster a collaborative work environment that promotes creativity and innovation. One way to do this is by leveraging the diverse perspectives and expertise of your team members to drive innovation. Collaboration helps bring different viewpoints to the table, which can lead to breakthrough ideas and solutions.

To effectively leverage diverse perspectives and expertise, you must first build a culture that values inclusivity and respect. Encourage open communication and feedback, and ensure that all team members have an equal opportunity to contribute their ideas. You should also provide training on cultural sensitivity and bias, as well as support for diverse hiring and promotion practices.

Another way to foster collaboration is through team-building exercises and activities. These can help team members develop a better understanding of each other's strengths, weaknesses, and communication styles, which can improve collaboration and increase the likelihood of success. Examples of team-building exercises include trust-building exercises, brainstorming sessions, and team-building retreats.

As a manager, it's also important to lead by example. You should model the desired behavior by actively seeking out and considering input from team members, and by acknowledging and rewarding their contributions. You should also encourage collaboration by recognizing and rewarding successful team efforts, and by promoting a culture that values cooperation over competition.

Technology can also be a powerful tool in promoting collaboration. Tools like virtual workspaces, online collaboration platforms, and project management software can help team members work together more efficiently and effectively. These tools can also facilitate communication and feedback, and help team members stay organized and on track.

In order to effectively leverage diverse perspectives and expertise, it's important to create a clear structure for collaboration. This includes defining roles and responsibilities, establishing clear goals and objectives, and providing the necessary resources and support. You should also develop a clear process for decision-making and conflict resolution, as well as a system for measuring progress and evaluating success.

Another key to leveraging diverse perspectives and expertise is to embrace failure as part of the learning process. Innovation often involves taking risks and trying new things, which can lead to failure. However, failure is also an opportunity to learn and improve, and it should be treated as such. Encourage your team to take risks and try new things, and create a culture that values experimentation and learning.

In addition to fostering collaboration within your own team, you should also look for opportunities to collaborate with other teams and departments within your organization. This can help to break down silos and promote cross-functional collaboration, which can lead to new ideas and solutions.

Finally, you should continually evaluate and adjust your approach to collaboration and innovation. This includes gathering feedback from team members, measuring success, and making adjustments as necessary. By staying open to feedback and continually looking for ways to improve, you can create a culture that promotes collaboration and drives innovation. To foster a culture of innovation, it is also important for managers to set clear goals and expectations for their teams. This means defining what success looks like, and providing a roadmap for how to achieve it. It also means setting specific metrics and key performance indicators (KPIs) to measure progress and ensure accountability.

Ultimately, the success of any collaborative innovation effort depends on the leadership and management skills of those in charge. Effective managers are those who are able to harness the power of collaboration, leverage diverse perspectives and expertise, and create an environment that supports innovation and experimentation. They are also able to communicate effectively, provide resources and support, set clear goals and expectations, and foster a culture of trust and respect among their team members.

Examples of companies that have successfully leveraged collaboration to drive innovation include Google, which is well-known for its innovative and collaborative culture. Google encourages its employees to share their ideas and provides a number of channels for collaboration, such as brainstorming sessions, hackathons, and cross-functional projects. Another example is IBM, which has a long history of collaboration and innovation. IBM's "InnovationJam" is a company-wide event that brings together employees from all over the world to brainstorm and share ideas.

Application

Adapting to Change and Embracing Innovation

Overview: Adapting to change and embracing innovation is essential for individuals and organizations to remain competitive in today's dynamic business environment. This application provides a set of tools and strategies to help individuals and teams manage change and leverage innovation to drive growth and success.

Features:

1. *Assess your current mindset:* This tool helps you identify your mindset and provides insights on how to develop a growth mindset to embrace change and innovation.

2. *Change management framework:* This feature provides a step-by-step approach for managing change, including communication strategies, managing resistance, and creating a plan for executing change.

3. *Creativity and experimentation toolkit:* This toolkit provides resources and tools to support experimentation and creative thinking. It includes techniques for brainstorming, idea generation, prototyping, and testing.

4. *Collaboration and team building tools:* This feature provides strategies and tools for building high-performing teams, including activities to build trust and collaboration.

Innovation metrics and evaluation: This feature provides tools for tracking innovation progress and evaluating the impact of innovation on business outcomes. It includes tools for measuring success, identifying challenges, and making adjustments to innovation strategies.

Benefits:

1. *Increase adaptability and resilience:* By using the tools and strategies in this application, individuals and teams can develop a growth mindset, build resilience, and embrace change as an opportunity for growth and innovation.

2. *Drive innovation:* The application provides a set of tools and resources to support creative thinking and experimentation, which helps individuals and teams generate new ideas and approaches to business challenges.

3. *Improve collaboration and teamwork:* The collaboration and team-building tools in the application can help teams build trust, communicate effectively, and work together to achieve common goals.

4. *Monitor and evaluate progress:* The innovation metrics and evaluation tools in the application help individuals and teams track progress and identify areas for improvement, which can lead to more effective and impactful innovation efforts.

5. *Enhance business outcomes:* By leveraging the tools and strategies in this application, individuals and organizations can achieve better business outcomes, including increased revenue, improved customer satisfaction, and a stronger competitive position in the market.

Overall, the Adapting to Change and Embracing Innovation application provides a comprehensive set of tools and strategies to help individuals and organizations navigate change and leverage innovation to achieve their goals. By using this application, individuals and teams can develop the mindset and skills necessary to succeed in today's rapidly changing business environment.

Summary

In summary, adapting to change and embracing innovation is crucial in today's dynamic and fast-paced business world. It requires a growth mindset, the ability to manage uncertainty and risk, create a culture of innovation, and leverage diverse perspectives and expertise. To adapt to change, employees must have a growth mindset that sees challenges as opportunities for growth. Resistance to change is common, but managing uncertainty and risk can help overcome these challenges. Communication and leadership play a critical role in managing change, and it is essential to create an environment that supports creativity and experimentation. Collaboration can drive innovation and leverage diverse perspectives and expertise to achieve better outcomes. Embracing experimentation and continuous improvement is also necessary for achieving success in today's rapidly evolving business environment. By implementing these strategies, businesses can adapt to change and remain competitive in the long term.

CHAPTER 10

Continuously Improving and
Developing as a Manager

The role of a manager is critical in any organization, and their ability to lead, motivate and guide teams is essential for the success of the company. However, to be a successful manager, it is not enough to rely on past experiences and knowledge. The best managers recognize the importance of continuous improvement and actively seek out opportunities to develop and refine their skills. In a fast-paced and ever-changing business environment, it is essential for managers to continuously improve their skills to adapt to new challenges and opportunities. Through ongoing learning and development, managers can gain the necessary tools and techniques to lead their teams effectively and make sound decisions in
complex situations.

The most effective managers are not content with simply maintaining the status quo. Instead, they are committed to continuously improving themselves and their teams. By setting high standards and consistently working to exceed them, they create a culture of excellence that benefits the entire organization. Continuous improvement is a core principle of modern management practices. As businesses strive for greater efficiency, productivity, and profitability, managers who embrace the philosophy of continuous improvement are better equipped to lead their teams to success. By constantly seeking out new ways to improve processes and workflows, managers can stay ahead of the curve and maintain a competitive edge. In the highly competitive world of business, the ability to learn and adapt is essential for success. Managers who are committed to ongoing development can position themselves as leaders in their field, demonstrating the skills and knowledge necessary to drive growth and innovation. By continually investing in themselves and their teams, these managers can achieve their full potential and take their organizations to new heights.

Being a manager is not an easy job. It requires a diverse set of skills, including leadership, communication, problem-solving, and strategic thinking. However, these skills are not fixed and can be continuously improved and developed. As the business world evolves, so do the demands placed on managers. Therefore, it is crucial for managers to continually learn and develop their skills to remain effective and competitive. In this context, continuously improving and developing as a manager is a crucial aspect of professional growth and success. In this chapter, we will explore the importance of ongoing learning and development for managers and provide some tips for how to continuously improve as a manager.

Strategies for Personal and Professional Growth as a Manager

As a manager, it's important to prioritize your personal and professional growth to stay relevant and effective in your role. To achieve this, one strategy is to seek out learning opportunities. This can involve attending industry conferences, taking online courses, or reading books on management and leadership. By actively pursuing new knowledge and skills, you can develop a well-rounded understanding of the latest trends and techniques in your field.

LinkedIn Learning is a powerful resource for managers looking to pursue learning opportunities and develop their skills. With LinkedIn Learning, you have access to a vast library of online courses covering a wide range of topics related to management and leadership. These courses are designed to help you acquire new knowledge and skills, and to stay up-to-date on the latest trends and best practices in your field.

One of the key advantages of LinkedIn Learning is its flexibility. You can access courses at any time, from any device, allowing you to fit learning into your busy schedule. Additionally, the courses are self-paced, so you can learn at your own speed and take as much time as you need to absorb the material.

Another benefit of LinkedIn Learning is that the courses are taught by experienced professionals and industry experts. This means that the content is up-to-date, relevant, and delivered by individuals with real-world experience in the field. In addition, many courses offer exercises, quizzes, and assessments to help you reinforce your learning and apply what you've learned to your job.

LinkedIn Learning also offers a variety of learning paths specifically designed for managers. These paths are curated collections of courses that are organized around specific skill sets, such as project management, communication, or leadership. By following a learning path, you can gain a deeper understanding of a particular area of management and develop the skills needed to excel in that area.

Overall, LinkedIn Learning is an excellent resource for managers looking to pursue personal and professional growth. With its wide range of courses, expert instructors, and flexible learning options, LinkedIn Learning can help managers stay up-to-date and develop the skills needed to excel in their roles.

Another important strategy for personal and professional growth is to seek out mentorship and feedback. Finding a mentor can provide valuable insights and guidance on how to navigate complex managerial challenges. Additionally, soliciting feedback from colleagues and team members can help you identify areas for improvement and refine your leadership style. This type of continuous feedback loop can be incredibly beneficial for refining your skills and growing as a manager.

Seeking out mentorship is a valuable strategy for managers who want to pursue professional growth. When seeking out a mentor, there are several key factors to consider to ensure that the relationship is effective and beneficial. One important factor is the compatibility of the mentor's experience with your own goals and needs. A mentor with experience in a different industry or area of management may still be valuable, but it's important to ensure that their knowledge and skills are relevant to your own career goals. For example, if you're a marketing manager looking to move into a leadership role, a mentor with experience in marketing leadership would be more valuable than a mentor with experience in finance.

Another important factor is chemistry and rapport between the mentor and mentee. It's important to find someone with whom you have a positive and productive relationship. This can make the mentoring experience more enjoyable and effective. This may require meeting with multiple potential mentors to find the right fit.

A successful mentorship relationship also requires mutual respect and trust. Both the mentor and mentee should be committed to the relationship and willing to invest time and effort in it. The mentee should be open to feedback and willing to act based on the mentor's advice, while the mentor should be committed to supporting the mentee's growth and development.

Effective communication is also critical in a mentorship relationship. The mentee should be able to articulate their goals and needs clearly, while the mentor should be able to provide feedback and guidance in a clear and constructive manner. This may involve setting specific goals and timelines for achieving them, and regularly checking in on progress.

It's important for the mentee to take an active role in the mentoring relationship. This means being prepared for meetings, actively seeking feedback, and following through on advice and guidance provided by the mentor. By taking an active role in the relationship, the mentee can maximize the benefits of the mentoring experience and accelerate their professional growth.

An often-overlooked aspect of personal and professional growth is self-care. As a manager, it's easy to get caught up in the demands of the job and neglect your own physical and emotional needs. However, taking care of yourself is critical to maintaining the energy and focus needed to be an effective leader. This can involve establishing healthy habits like exercise, meditation, or simply taking breaks throughout the workday to recharge.

Networking is another important strategy for personal and professional growth as a manager. Building strong relationships with peers in your industry can help you stay up-to-date on the latest trends and developments in your field. It can also open up new opportunities for collaboration and growth, both personally and professionally. Attending industry events, joining professional organizations, and engaging on social media are all great ways to expand your network and build meaningful relationships.

Networking is a powerful tool that managers can leverage to pursue personal and professional growth. By building strong relationships with peers in their industry, managers can stay up-to-date on the latest trends and developments in their field. They can also discover new opportunities for collaboration, mentorship, and growth, both personally and professionally.

One effective way to network is by attending industry events such as conferences, workshops, and seminars. These events provide a valuable opportunity to meet and connect with others in your field, learn about the latest trends and best practices, and showcase your own knowledge and skills. By engaging with others at these events, you can establish new connections and build relationships that can last long after the event is over.

Another way to network is by joining professional organizations or associations. These groups provide a sense of community and support, as well as access to industry-specific resources, events, and training. By becoming an active member of a professional organization, you can connect with others who share your interests and goals, and leverage their experience and knowledge to accelerate your own growth and development.

Social media platforms such as LinkedIn, Twitter, and Facebook also provide powerful opportunities for networking. By engaging with others on these platforms, you can build relationships with people across the globe, and stay up-to-date on the latest industry news and trends. You can also share your own insights and perspectives, and showcase your expertise and experience to a broader audience.

Networking is an essential strategy for managers looking to pursue personal and professional growth. By attending industry events, joining professional organizations, and engaging on social media, managers can expand their network, build meaningful relationships, and discover new opportunities for collaboration and growth. By investing time and effort in networking, managers can position themselves for long-term success in their field.

Finally, it's important to approach personal and professional growth with a growth mindset. This means embracing challenges as opportunities to learn and grow, rather than seeing them as obstacles to overcome. By cultivating a growth mindset, you can approach your work with a sense of curiosity and open-mindedness that will allow you to continuously develop your skills and capabilities as a manager.

Maximizing Leadership Potential through Ongoing Development

Maximizing leadership potential through ongoing development is a critical strategy for managers who want to stay ahead of the curve and succeed in their careers. By continuously learning and improving, managers can expand their skillset, build resilience, and develop new strategies for leading their teams and organizations.

One of the key ways managers can maximize their leadership potential is by seeking out ongoing professional development opportunities. This can include attending workshops and seminars, pursuing advanced degrees or certifications, and engaging in on-the-job training and mentoring. By continuously learning and growing, managers can stay ahead of the curve and become more effective leaders.

Another important strategy for maximizing leadership potential is developing a growth mindset. This means adopting a belief that skills and abilities can be developed through dedication and hard work. With a growth mindset, managers are more likely to embrace challenges, learn from failure, and persist in the face of setbacks. This can help managers develop resilience, build confidence, and maximize their leadership potential.

Effective communication is another critical skill for maximizing leadership potential. Managers who communicate clearly, effectively, and empathetically are more likely to build strong relationships with their teams and stakeholders, and navigate challenging situations with ease. By continuously honing their communication skills, managers can become more effective leaders and build high-performing teams.

Building strong relationships with stakeholders is another important factor for maximizing leadership potential. This includes not only building relationships with direct reports, but also with peers, superiors, clients, and other stakeholders. By building strong relationships, managers can gain trust, build consensus, and make better decisions. This can help managers lead more effectively and achieve their goals.

A key strategy for maximizing leadership potential is developing a sense of purpose and direction. Effective leaders are driven by a sense of purpose and a clear vision of where they want to go. By developing a sense of purpose, managers can align their efforts with their organization's goals, build passion and motivation, and inspire others to follow their lead. This can help managers maximize their leadership potential and make a meaningful impact in their field.

Attending professional development workshops and conferences is a key strategy for managers who want to improve their skills and stay up-to-date on the latest trends and best practices in their field. These events provide valuable opportunities for learning, networking, and professional growth.

One of the key benefits of attending professional development events is the opportunity to learn from experts in your field. Many conferences and workshops feature keynote speakers, panels, and breakout sessions where attendees can learn about the latest research, trends, and strategies from leaders in their field. This can provide valuable insights and perspectives that can help managers improve their own skills and approach to management.

In addition to learning from experts, attending professional development events is also a great way to learn from peers in your field. Conferences and workshops provide a unique opportunity to connect with other managers, share ideas and experiences, and build a network of supportive colleagues. By engaging with others in your field, you can gain new insights, learn from others' experiences, and build meaningful relationships that can support your long-term growth and success.

Attending professional development events can also help managers stay up-to-date on the latest trends and best practices in their field. By attending workshops and conferences, managers can learn about new tools, techniques, and strategies that can help them better manage their teams and organizations. This can help managers stay ahead of the curve and position themselves as leaders in their field.

Another key benefit of attending professional development events is the opportunity to gain new perspectives and ideas. By attending workshops and conferences, managers can learn about new approaches to management, as well as different ways of thinking about challenges and opportunities. This can help managers break out of their own echo chamber and expand their horizons, opening up new opportunities for growth and development.

Overall, attending professional development workshops and conferences is an essential strategy for managers who want to improve their skills, stay up-to-date on the latest trends, and position themselves for long-term success in their field. By investing in professional development, managers can gain new insights, learn from experts and peers, and build a network of supportive colleagues who can help them achieve their goals.

While attending professional development workshops and conferences can be highly beneficial for managers seeking personal and professional growth, there are also several pitfalls to avoid. Here are some common pitfalls to keep in mind:

1. *Overcommitting:* With so many workshops and sessions to choose from, it can be tempting to try to attend everything. However, overcommitting can lead to burnout and can dilute the impact of the workshops and sessions you do attend. It's important to carefully review the schedule and choose the sessions that align with your goals and interests.

2. *Failing to Follow Up:* Attending a workshop or conference is just the first step. To truly benefit from the experience, it's important to follow up with the connections you make and the insights you gain. This can include following up with speakers, reaching out to new contacts, and taking action on what you've learned.

3. *Ignoring the Basics:* While attending a workshop or conference can be an exciting opportunity, it's important not to forget the basics. This includes things like getting enough sleep, staying

hydrated, and taking breaks when needed. Ignoring these basics can lead to burnout and can undermine the benefits of attending the event.

4. *Focusing too much on Networking:* While networking is an important aspect of attending a professional development event, it's important not to focus on it to the exclusion of everything else. The primary goal of attending a workshop or conference should be to learn and grow. Networking should be seen as a means to that end, rather than an end in itself.

Not Preparing Ahead of Time: To get the most out of a workshop or conference, it's important to come prepared. This can include reading up on the speakers and topics in advance, reviewing the schedule, and setting goals for what you want to get out of the event. By coming prepared, you'll be better equipped to engage with the material and make the most of the experience.

Techniques for Continuous Improvement in Management Skills

Effective management requires a combination of skills, including communication, decision-making, problem-solving, and leadership. Managers who want to continuously improve their management skills can adopt a number of techniques to enhance their effectiveness.

One technique for continuous improvement is seeking out feedback. Asking colleagues, employees, and superiors for constructive feedback can help managers identify areas for improvement and refine their skills. This can also help managers build stronger relationships with their teams and stakeholders, by showing a willingness to listen and adapt to feedback.

Another technique for continuous improvement is setting specific goals. By setting clear goals for what they want to achieve, managers can focus their efforts and measure their progress. This can help managers stay motivated and accountable, and can also provide a sense of direction for their team.

Regular reflection is another technique for continuous improvement. By taking the time to reflect on their experiences and actions, managers can identify strengths and weaknesses, learn from past mistakes, and develop new strategies for managing their team. This can also help managers stay attuned to their values and goals, and ensure they are aligned with their organization's mission.

Training and development are also important techniques for continuous improvement. Managers who attend workshops, conferences, and training sessions can learn new skills and gain exposure to new ideas and approaches. This can help them stay up-to-date on the latest trends and best practices, and can also help them connect with other professionals in their field.

Finally, mentorship is another powerful technique for continuous improvement. Seeking out a mentor who can provide guidance, feedback, and advice can help managers refine their skills and gain new perspectives on their work. This can also help managers build a strong professional network and gain exposure to new opportunities and ideas.

By adopting these techniques for continuous improvement, managers can enhance their effectiveness and build a strong foundation for long-term success. Whether through seeking feedback, setting goals, reflection, training and development, or mentorship, there are a wide range of strategies managers can use to refine their skills and continue to grow as leaders.

Staying Ahead of the Curve

Advancing Your Management Capabilities

Staying ahead of the curve in today's fast-paced business environment is essential for managers who want to succeed. Here are 10 strategies for advancing your management capabilities:

1. Develop a growth mindset: A growth mindset is the belief that one's abilities and skills can be developed through dedication and hard work. By adopting a growth mindset, managers can focus on continuous improvement and develop a strong sense of resilience.

2. Seek out feedback: Feedback is essential for improving your management capabilities. Seek feedback from your team, colleagues, and superiors to identify areas for improvement and refine your skills.

3. Embrace new technologies: New technologies are constantly emerging, and managers who want to stay ahead of the curve need to embrace these innovations. Invest in new tools and platforms

that can help you streamline your work and improve your team's productivity.

4. Learn from your mistakes: Mistakes are inevitable, but they can also be a valuable learning experience. Instead of dwelling on your mistakes, take the time to reflect on what went wrong and identify ways to improve.

5. Build a strong professional network: Building a strong professional network can help you stay up-to-date on the latest trends and best practices, and can also provide you with new opportunities and insights.

6. Take on new challenges: Taking on new challenges can help you expand your skill set and gain exposure to new ideas and approaches. Look for opportunities to take on new projects or responsibilities that will stretch your capabilities.

7. Attend conferences and training sessions: Attending conferences and training sessions can provide you with exposure to new ideas and approaches, as well as an opportunity to network with other professionals in your field.

8. Foster a culture of innovation: Encouraging your team to think creatively and embrace new ideas can help you stay ahead of the curve. Foster a culture of innovation by rewarding risk-taking and promoting collaboration.

9. Stay up-to-date on industry trends: Staying up-to-date on the latest trends and best practices in your industry is essential for staying ahead of the curve. Read industry publications, attend webinars, and participate in industry forums to stay informed.

10. Continuously refine your communication skills: Effective communication is essential for successful management. Continuously refine your communication skills by seeking feedback, practicing active listening, and being clear and concise in your messages.

Staying ahead of the curve requires a combination of personal and professional development. By adopting a growth mindset, seeking feedback, embracing new technologies, learning from mistakes, building a strong professional network, taking on new challenges, attending conferences and training sessions, fostering a culture of innovation, staying up-to-date on industry trends, and continuously refining your communication skills, managers can enhance their capabilities and position themselves for long-term success.

Cultivating a Growth Mindset

Nurturing Your Evolution as a Manager

Cultivating a growth mindset is essential for managers who want to continue to evolve and develop in their role. Here are five key strategies for nurturing your evolution as a manager and developing a growth mindset.

Embrace challenges: Instead of shying away from challenges, view them as an opportunity for growth. Seek out new challenges that push you out of your comfort zone, and approach them with a positive and open mindset.

Embracing challenges is a critical mindset for managers who want to continue to grow and develop in their role. Instead of avoiding challenges or sticking to familiar tasks and routines, managers should actively seek out new challenges that push them outside of their comfort zone. This can include taking on new projects, working with new teams, or tackling complex problems.

When facing a challenge, it's important to approach it with a positive and open mindset. Instead of viewing the challenge as a threat or obstacle, see it as an opportunity for growth and development. By embracing challenges, managers can develop new skills, expand their knowledge base, and gain valuable experience that will help them succeed in their role.

To effectively embrace challenges, managers should be willing to take risks and try new things. This may involve stepping outside of their comfort zone or doing things differently than they have in the past. It's also important to maintain a positive attitude and remain open to feedback and learning opportunities.

By embracing challenges, managers can cultivate a growth mindset that will help them achieve long-term success. This mindset encourages continuous learning, development, and improvement, and helps managers to stay adaptable and resilient in the face of change and uncertainty.

Learn from failures: Rather than seeing failures as a setback, view them as a learning opportunity. Analyze what went wrong and identify ways to improve for the next time.

Learning from failures is an important skill for managers who want to continue to grow and develop in their role. Instead of seeing failures as a setback or personal shortcoming, managers should view them as a valuable learning opportunity.

To learn from failures, it's important to analyze what went wrong and identify the root cause of the problem. This may involve gathering feedback from colleagues, reviewing data or performance metrics, or reflecting on personal behavior or decisions. Once the root cause has been identified, managers can then develop a plan to address the issue and prevent it from happening in the future.

It's important to approach failures with a growth mindset, rather than a fixed mindset. A growth mindset allows managers to view setbacks as opportunities for learning and improvement, while a fixed mindset may lead to a fear of failure and a reluctance to take risks or try new things. To effectively learn from failures, it's also important to maintain a positive attitude and seek out support from colleagues, mentors, or other trusted advisors. This can help managers to gain perspective and identify new strategies for overcoming challenges and achieving success.

By learning from failures, managers can develop new skills, improve their decision-making abilities, and gain valuable experience that will help them succeed in their role. By embracing a growth mindset and seeing failures as opportunities for learning and growth, managers can continue to evolve and develop in their role and achieve long-term success.

Seek out feedback: Feedback is a critical tool for personal and professional growth. Ask for feedback from colleagues, superiors, and subordinates to help identify areas of strength and areas for improvement.

Seeking out feedback is an important practice for managers who want to continue to grow and develop in their role. Feedback can provide valuable insight into areas of strength and areas for improvement, as well as help managers to gain a better understanding of how their behavior and decisions are perceived by others.

To effectively seek out feedback, managers should be proactive in asking for feedback from colleagues, superiors, and subordinates. This may involve scheduling regular check-ins or performance reviews, seeking out feedback after a specific project or event, or simply asking for feedback on an ongoing basis.

It's important to approach feedback with an open and non-defensive attitude. Rather than becoming defensive or dismissive of feedback that may be critical or challenging, managers should listen actively and ask clarifying questions to gain a better understanding of the feedback being provided.

Once feedback has been received, it's important to take action on the feedback by identifying specific areas for improvement and developing a plan to address them. This may involve seeking out additional training or support, working with a mentor or coach, or simply focusing on improving specific behaviors or skills.

By seeking out feedback, managers can gain valuable insight into how their behavior and decisions are perceived by others, identify areas for improvement, and continue to develop and grow in their role. This practice can also help to build stronger relationships with colleagues and foster a culture of open communication and continuous improvement.

Engage in continuous learning: Commit to continuous learning by reading industry publications, attending conferences, participating in online courses and training, and seeking out mentorship opportunities.

Engaging in continuous learning is an important practice for managers who want to stay up-to-date on the latest trends and developments in their field, as well as develop new skills and knowledge that can help them succeed in their role. One way to engage in continuous learning is to read industry publications, such as trade journals, academic journals, and online news sources. These publications can provide valuable insights into emerging trends, best practices, and case studies that can help managers to stay ahead of the curve.

Attending conferences and other industry events is another way to engage in continuous learning. These events provide opportunities to hear from experts in the field, network with colleagues, and gain new insights and perspectives on the challenges facing the industry.

Online courses and training programs can also be an effective way to engage in continuous learning. These programs can provide flexible and accessible opportunities to develop new skills and knowledge, and may be available at little or no cost.

Seeking out mentorship opportunities is another important way to engage in continuous learning. Working with a mentor can provide valuable guidance and support, as well as an opportunity to learn from someone with more experience and expertise in the field.

By committing to continuous learning, managers can develop new skills and knowledge that can help them succeed in their role, stay up-to-date on the latest trends and developments in their field, and continue to grow and develop as a professional. This practice can also help to build a culture of learning and innovation within the organization, as managers share their knowledge and insights with colleagues and work to identify new opportunities for growth and improvement.

Focus on progress, not perfection: Perfectionism can be a major barrier to growth and development. Instead of focusing on achieving perfection, strive for progress and incremental improvement over time.

Focusing on progress instead of perfection is an important practice for managers who want to continue to grow and develop in their role. Perfectionism can be a major barrier to progress, as it can create unrealistic expectations and prevent managers from taking risks and making mistakes.

Instead of striving for perfection, managers should focus on making progress and incremental improvements over time. This approach can help managers to build momentum and make steady progress towards their goals, while also allowing them to learn from their mistakes and adjust their approach as needed.

To focus on progress, managers should set achievable goals and break them down into smaller, manageable steps. This can help to create a sense of momentum and progress, as managers can see tangible progress towards their goals on a regular basis.

Managers should also celebrate their successes and acknowledge their progress, even if it may seem small. Recognizing progress can help to build confidence and motivation, which can in turn lead to further growth and development.

At the same time, it's important for managers to learn from their mistakes and failures. Instead of viewing mistakes as setbacks, managers should see them as opportunities to learn and improve. By taking the time to reflect on what went wrong and identifying ways to improve, managers can continue to make progress and grow in their role.

By focusing on progress instead of perfection, managers can build a growth mindset that allows them to continue to learn and develop over time. This approach can help to create a culture of continuous improvement and innovation within the organization, as managers are encouraged to take risks, learn from their mistakes, and work towards achieving their goals.

By embracing a growth mindset and focusing on personal and professional development, managers can continue to evolve and improve in their role. Remember to be open to new challenges, learn from failures, seek out feedback, engage in continuous learning, and focus on progress rather than perfection. By doing so, you'll be able to cultivate a growth mindset that will help you achieve long-term success.

Application

Here are some ideas for managers to continuously improve and develop their skills:

1. Attend professional development workshops and conferences: Managers can attend workshops and conferences related to their industry to learn new skills and stay up-to-date with the latest trends.

2. Seek out mentorship: Managers can seek out a mentor who can provide guidance and support for their professional development.

3. Build a strong network: Managers can attend industry events, join professional organizations, and engage on social media to expand their network and build meaningful relationships.

4. Engage in continuous learning: Managers can read industry publications, participate in online courses and training, and seek out mentorship opportunities to stay ahead of the curve.

5. Foster a growth mindset: Managers can embrace challenges, learn from failures, seek out feedback, and focus on progress rather than perfection to foster a growth mindset.

6. Solicit feedback: Managers can ask for feedback from colleagues, superiors, and subordinates to help identify areas of strength and areas for improvement.

7. Set goals and track progress: Managers can set specific goals for their professional development and track their progress over time to stay motivated and focused.

8. Take on new challenges: Managers can take on new challenges and projects that push them out of their comfort zone to develop new skills and capabilities.

9. Build a culture of learning: Managers can encourage their team to engage in continuous learning and provide opportunities for professional development to foster a culture of learning.

Engage in self-reflection: Managers can engage in regular self-reflection to identify areas of strength and areas for improvement, and take proactive steps to develop their skills and capabilities.

Summary

As a manager, it is important to continuously improve and develop your skills and knowledge to effectively lead your team and achieve organizational goals. Here are some ideas for managers to consider:

1. Seek feedback: Regularly ask for feedback from your team, peers, and superiors to identify areas for improvement and build on your strengths.

2. Take courses or attend workshops: Look for training opportunities that can help you build your skills in areas such as leadership, communication, and project management.

3. Read and research: Keep up-to-date on the latest industry trends and management strategies by reading books, articles, and blogs.

4. Mentor or be mentored: Consider participating in a mentorship program, either as a mentor or mentee, to gain new perspectives and insights.

5. Attend conferences or networking events: Attend industry conferences or networking events to learn from other professionals and build your professional network.

6. Set goals and track progress: Set specific goals for your personal and professional development and track your progress over time.

7. Collaborate with others: Work with your team, peers, and superiors to identify opportunities for collaboration and knowledge sharing.

8. Embrace challenges: Look for challenging projects and assignments that push you out of your comfort zone and help you grow.

By consistently working to improve and develop their skills, managers can become more effective leaders and drive their teams to success.

Made in the USA
Monee, IL
06 December 2024

72691450R00095